Praise for
GOING
sane

"Phillips has made psychoanalytic thought li̶ ̶ ̶ ̶ ̶ ̶more poetic than ever. . . . One of [his] finest and most broadly appealing books." —*New York Times*

"Phillips offers a detailed description of what sanity can mean today." —*Los Angeles Times*

"Phillips is one of the finest prose stylists at work in the language, an Emerson for our time." —John Banville

"Beautifully written . . . clever and funny and properly profound. . . . A lovely addition to Phillips's guides to living a happier life."
—*GQ*

"In classic psychoanalytic style, Phillips strips our lives down to the fundamentals to illustrate the delicate balance between sanity and insanity. His arguments, both thought-provoking and provocative, may affect future definitions of sanity and madness, and readers are left with a fresh awareness of what it really means to be sane."
—*Publishers Weekly*

"Phillips radiates infectious charm. The brew of gaiety, compassion, exuberance and idealism is heady and disarming."
—Roy Porter

"A recent spate of work in positive psychology has extended the discipline beyond its traditional occupation with staving off the negative. Adam Phillips's book asks that we question the gap between being not insane and being sane. As surely as vanilla is a flavor, sanity is a property, and this book delineates its parameters with considerable erudition."
—Andrew Solomon, author of *The Noonday Demon*, winner of the National Book Award

"In *Going Sane*, Adam Phillips, writing with his usual aphoristic vigor and humorous gleam, once again undertakes to examine the convenient untruths—the 'mostly tacit preferences and assumptions'—by which we live. This time around his subject is sanity itself. He probes and pokes at this necessary but ill-defined term, drawing on a range of psychoanalytic and literary references—including D. W. Winnicott, F. Scott Fitzgerald, R. D. Laing, and Wordsworth—asking improbable but intuitively correct questions: whether, for instance, there is such a thing as sane violence; what constitutes 'normal' as opposed to 'false' sanity; and what sane sex might look like. He is, as ever, an original and lucid spirit, a buzzing intellectual gadfly in the ointment of our easy answers."

—Daphne Merkin, author of *Dreaming of Hitler: Passions and Provocations*

"Adam Phillips has written an extraordinarily generous and subtle book on a most inevitable and necessary (and yet surprising) subject: the nature of sanity. Who wouldn't want to read this book—now more than ever? It is written as if to be overheard—quiet and explosive. Its sentences pack in so much epigrammatic wisdom, cleanly and effortlessly, one feels, in the very marrow of the writing, a sensation one could best describe as, well, sanity. What a beautiful, unfussily important, and emotionally brilliant book."

—Jorie Graham, Pulitzer Prize–winning author of *The Dream of the Unified Field*

"A probing exploration of the full meaning of sanity. . . . Challenges the reader to reconsider the taken-for-granted notion that sanity is just another word for mental health." —*Kirkus Reviews*

"Well-argued and stunningly thought-provoking. Phillips has tackled a 'big idea' in a sophisticated yet spirited way." —*Library Journal*

"[Phillips] is the closest thing we have to a philosopher of happiness." —*The Observer* (London)

© Toby Glanville

About the Author

ADAM PHILLIPS is a psychoanalyst and the author of eleven previous books, including *Side Effects*; *On Kissing, Tickling, and Being Bored*; *On Flirtation*; *Darwin's Worms*; and *Houdini's Box*. He writes regularly for the *New York Times*, the *London Review of Books*, and *The Observer*, and is general editor of the new Penguin Modern Classics translations of Freud. He lives in London.

ADAM PHILLIPS

GOING
sane

HARPER PERENNIAL

NEW YORK • LONDON • TORONTO • SYDNEY

HARPER ● PERENNIAL

First published in Great Britain in 2005 by Hamish Hamilton, an imprint of
Penguin Books.

A hardcover edition of this book was published in 2005 by Fourth Estate,
an imprint of HarperCollins Publishers.

FIRST HARPER PERENNIAL EDITION PUBLISHED 2007.

Designed by Cassandra J. Pappas

The Library of Congress has catalogued the hardcover edition as follows:

Phillips, Adam.
    Going sane: maps of happiness/Adam Phillips.
        p.   cm.
    ISBN-10: 0-00-715539-5
    ISBN-13: 978-0-00-715539-2
    1. Mental health—Philosophy,   2. Psychiatry—Philosophy.
    3. Psychoanalysis.   I. Title.

    RC437.5.P435   2005
    616.89—dc22   2005040063

ISBN: 978-0-00-715536-1 (pbk.)
ISBN-13: 0-00-715536-0 (pbk.)

07 08 09 10 11 WBT/QF 10 9 8 7 6 5 4 3 2 1

for Judith

. . . if, by some mischance, people understood each other, they would never be able to reach agreement.

—CHARLES BAUDELAIRE, *Intimate Journals*

Contents

Preface

When the press reported in 2003 that "a US court of appeal [*sic*] has ruled that a death row prisoner be forcibly treated for psychosis which would make him sane enough to be executed" (*Guardian*, November 2) no one reading the report would have been too baffled by the intended meaning. Charles Singleton, the report continued, "who stabbed a shopworker to death in 1979, believes his prison cell is possessed by demons, that a prison doctor implanted a device in his ear and that he is both God and the supreme court."

"Sane enough to be executed" presumably means, in this context, sentient enough, responsible enough, guilty enough to experience the punishment as punishment rather than as something else; if Singleton does believe that he is God and the Supreme Court, he could, for example, see himself as having taken justice into his own hands, as having redeemed himself. His sanity, should the treatment work, would be reflected in his being more in touch with consensual reality; able to acknowledge both what he had done, and that what he had done was punishable. In an extreme case such as this, the madness being referred to—"Singleton was diagnosed as a paranoid schizophrenic in 1983"—seems no more contentious than the sanity that is being appealed to. And yet the phrase "sane enough to be executed" serves to remind us just what we might lose if the word "sanity" no longer made sense to us. It gathers up, in its own furtive way, a vast number of mostly tacit preferences and assumptions, of prejudices and ideals about what we think we should be, or should be like when we are at our best. It also assures us at the same time that there is a "we" that exists by virtue of its commitment to this value ("we" know what the phrase "sane enough to be executed" must mean): that we can be agents of intentions and motives that can be understood by others and ourselves; that we can take responsibility for our actions and their (often unknowable) consequences; that we can consent to being governed by certain laws and rules and regulations; that we can be realistic about our needs, and meet them without doing too much harm to other people. This might be the kind of sanity that Singleton needs in order to be properly executed. But it is rare, as we shall see, for sanity to be defined; more often than not it is referred to without its meaning ever being spelled out. Charles Singleton may be "psychotic," a "paranoid schizophrenic," but what would it really mean for him to be sane enough to be executed?

A WORD WITH few synonyms, "sanity" has always been an unfashionable term that has never quite gone out of fashion. First used by physicians in the seventeenth century to refer to "health in body and mind," its more familiar modern connotation as the opposite of or antidote to madness only really developed, as we shall see, in the nineteenth century. It was a word taken up by the new mind-doctors and mental hygienists, but never systematically studied or defined. Even though people never collected examples of it, or scientifically researched it, or found it in foreign countries; even though it was rarely described, unlike madness, with any great gusto or commitment, and as a word was (and is) rarely found in poems, titles, proverbs, advertisements or jokes; even though it is a word with virtually no scientific credibility, and of little literary use, it has become a necessary term. Exactly what it has been necessary for—and indeed what, if anything, it might be necessary for in the future—is the subject of this book.

By the late 1970s, when I began my psychoanalytic training, the glamorization of madness—the promotion of madness as revelation, as political protest, as the higher sanity—was rarely spoken of. The antipsychiatrists of the 1960s, with their commitment to therapeutic communities rather than mental hospitals, and their understanding of mental illness as existential crisis rather than malingering or neurological disorder, had seen madness as a quest for personal authenticity. Their therapeutic project was not to get people back to normal, but to show them how the need to be normal had driven them crazy. But the libertarian hopes of these radical therapists, like so many of the fresh hopes of the 1960s, proved to be short-lived. A decade later, and the casualties of the antipsychiatry movement were often more vocal, and more poignant, than its defenders. What the antipsychiatrists— most notably R. D. Laing and David Cooper in practice, and Michel Foucault and Jean-Paul Sartre in theory— were rightly promoting was that the so-called mad had something to say, and that it was worth listening to and taking seriously. Instead of incarcerating disturbing people in diagnoses and institutions, they suggested that we should start wondering where we had got our ideas about normality from. The very word "mad" needed to be rescued from the cruelty that was invested in its pejorative connotations. The villains of the antipsychiatry worldview were those all too scientific psychiatrists who were committed to the militant cure and control of anyone who behaved frighteningly badly; the heros and heroines were those who took the mad on their own terms, and who understood the language of the mad as anguished, accurate personal (and therefore political) history. The question was: who is most worth listening to, the experts on insanity or the insane themselves? And, of course, what is it that the insane are equipped to tell us about— the human condition (albeit at its most extreme) or just the experience of the unlucky few? For the antipsychiatrists there was no them-and-us: everyone was in a certain sense mad. For the often demonized psychiatrists there were the sane and the mad, and they could tell the difference. That, in effect, was what a psychiatrist was: someone who could tell the mad from the sane.

What the psychiatrists and the antipsychiatrists of the 1960s and 1970s had acknowledged in their quite different ways was that there is a tremendous fear in our culture about madness. But it is striking, in retrospect, that there has been no particular enthusiasm for the idea of sanity. Erich Fromm's *The Sane Society* (1956) was more of an elegy for the possibility of sanity in capitalist societies than anything else. R. D. Laing and Aaron Esterson's classic *Sanity, Madness and the Family* (1964) was entirely about how certain kinds of family life drive people crazy; Thomas Szasz's celebrated *The Myth of Mental Illness* (1960) had little to say about whether there is a compara-

ble myth of mental health. And even the voluminous literature on child development that came after the trauma
of the Second World War had no interest in the child's
sanity per se; the focus as ever was on pathology, on what
could go wrong in a child's life, and how to recognize it.
There were many competing accounts of what it meant
for a life to go wrong. But the sense you would get from
reading most of the so-called professional literature, as I
did then, was that, for more and more people, life didn't
work. Both the apocalyptic fervor of the antipsychiatrists
and the sober, supposed realism of the scientists combined to make the whole notion of sanity seem somehow
irrelevant. There was too much unhappiness, too much
madness to talk about.

Most of the parents I saw as a child psychotherapist
working in schools, hospitals and child-guidance clinics in
the 1970s and 1980s were worried that their children,
whatever their symptoms, were in some way mad; and virtually all the adolescents I saw believed they must be going
mad to be feeling as they did. This was true across all
classes and generations. It was as though any unintelligible
kind of suffering was the first sign of a madness that was
always looming; that people had come to believe in their
potential to be mad. Clearly, the controversies of the 1960s
and 1970s about psychiatry and the nature of mental illness were as much about the modern fear of madness—

both what might be done about that fear, and what that fear might be a fear of—as about its definition. It is a strange irony that even though madness has terrorized us more now than ever before—or perhaps because it has—we have been unable to give persuasive accounts of what sanity might be, and why it still might matter to us. This book is an attempt to reopen our account.

In Part One, "The Suspicion of the Thing," I give what amounts to notes toward the definition of sanity. Notes not merely because the history of our ideas about sanity is virtually undocumented, but because there is something about the whole notion of sanity that seems to make us averse to defining it. Unlike madness, sanity doesn't make people write well about it, or even want to. The best definitions we have, as is often the case once we look outside the more official histories of science, are the uses the word has been put to by imaginative writers. We can learn more, as I try to show, from the way Shakespeare uses the word in *Hamlet,* or Orwell uses it in *1984,* than its more tendentious, more professionally coercive uses in the mental health literature, which has a vested interest in its more specific definitions. People have written, in English, from the seventeenth century onward with great authority and conviction about pathology and diagnosis and, indeed, about the history of madness. Sanity has been equivalently underdescribed, which is why its casual use can be as revealing as its more concerned use. It is worth wondering why, given the sheer scale of contemporary unhappiness, there are no accounts of what a sane life would look like. Or of why a sane life might be more worth living than, say, a happy life, or a healthy life, or a successful life.

In Part Two, "Making the Case," I look at both how bewitched we are by madness, by a prevailing story that comes in many forms that we are essentially mad, bad and dangerous to know; and at how we have to tease out from the available modern accounts of madness and badness what it might mean to be sane. Because of this background belief that we have much to fear about ourselves—which, of course, has a distinguished history, and a great deal of contemporary evidence to support it—the sanity is hard to find. But if the sanity is hard to find, the hope may be too. The possibility of there being at least sane versions of ourselves has traditionally been the source of our hopes for ourselves; and the idea of sanity, in which we have invested so much, has always been something that we could, at least, look forward to. I want to suggest in this part that sanity has been one of the more difficult, more perplexing ideals that we have come up with for ourselves. Whether it is an object of desire, something one could devote one's life to achieving, something one could feel passionate about, or whether, more modestly, it may just be one of our better states of mind—like a voice inside us, fleeting but occasionally available for comment—sanity may not be as easy as we might wish to recognize or to agree upon.

Even to consider, as I do in this part, how to rear a sane child, or what a sane sexual life would be like; or, perhaps even more bewilderingly now, what it would be like to have a sane attitude toward money, is to realize just how much sanity—if it is something we aim at—has to be aimed at without a target. Whether, for example, there is such a thing as sane violence has become perhaps our most pressing political concern. Most people don't want to be insane about such important matters, and yet the alternatives to insanity about these issues are not quite clear. It is one of the contentions of Part Two, and indeed of the book, that sanity is at once something we resist and something we are prone to doubt the existence of. Those of us who don't find madness inspiring are surprisingly short of options; and, at present, there is not much help available. Self-help books aspire to assist us, but they usually take it for granted that in the areas of our lives that matter, we are always capable of making choices. One way or another they all try to restore our confidence in our willpower. But madness, of course, has less reassuring stories to tell about our so-called self-control, about our talent or even our willingness to design our own lives.

And sanity seems to tell us very few stories about itself, about what there is about us that can deal with this madness. There are no modern utopian stories that tell us how we might live in a way that would make the fear of madness disappear. In other words, as this part points out, even though it would seem to be against common sense, we know where we are with madness, whereas sanity confounds us.

It should matter to us, especially now, that sanity is something we can't get excited about; that it so rarely figures among our contemporary aspirations. It is possible that in losing heart about our sanity—in not describing or addressing it—we are losing more than we realize. It means, even at its most minimal, that we are becoming extremely narrow-minded about what we want, about imagining possibilities for ourselves. Imagining possibilities for ourselves involves telling stories about what we think we are like, what we think we want, and what we think we are capable of. We need these conjectures that attempt to blend our wishes with reality to keep us going. But above all we need conjectures that are persuasive in a way that rouses people to counter and complement them. So the final part, "Sane Now," is a stab at sanity; a hope that giving a contemporary account of sanity might invite further competing accounts. We need an alternative now to wealth, happiness, security and long life as the main constituents of a Good Life. To think about sanity as a different kind of prosperity, as a realistic hope rather than a merely bland or (austerely) grand alternative to madness, is an opportunity, I think, to include in our accounts of a Good Life for ourselves both the unpredictable effect on us of our histories—both what we have experienced ourselves and the illimitable experience of previous generations—and the urgencies and vulnerabilities of our biological destinies. It would be sane now to work out how we have become the only animals who can't bear themselves; and how, if at all, we might become the animals who can.

PART one

The Suspicion of the Thing: Notes Toward the Definition of Sanity

PEOPLE HAVE USUALLY wondered whether Hamlet was mad, not whether he was sane. The word itself—derived from the Latin *sanus* and the French *sain*, and meaning originally of the body . . . "healthy, sound, not diseased"—was not commonly used in the seventeenth century, when it first appeared. It is, indeed, used only once by Shakespeare, and perhaps unsurprisingly in *Hamlet;* and, also perhaps unsurprisingly, it is used by Polonius. Polonius wonders, like several other people in the play, whether Hamlet is "mad," a word used over two hundred times by Shakespeare; and used, with its cognate "madness," thirty-five times in *Hamlet*. The words "mad" and "madness" are bandied about in *Hamlet* (though not often by Hamlet himself) because they seem pertinent— they seem to locate a problem without quite saying what the problem is. The madness resists definition—no one is quite sure what it refers to, or indeed what Hamlet himself seems to be referring to. Characters in the play often

don't understand what Hamlet is saying, but Hamlet reassures them that they do, at least, understand what they
themselves are saying. "Mad," in the play, is a word for
"puzzling." "Your noble son is mad," Polonius says help-
fully to Gertrude and Claudius: "Mad call I it. For, to define true madness, What is't but to be nothing else than
mad? But let that go" (II.2.92–5). Polonius clearly has a
problem about definition here; "true madness" is a
strange phrase since madness is a form of dissembling.
True madness, for example, could just mean acting. We
might wonder whether Hamlet is pretending to wonder
about the difference between selves on show in public
and selves on show in private. Madness, in other words,
tends to the theatrical, even when it is not good theater.
Sanity tends the other way. Being mad, as Polonius suggests, can mean acting as if one were mad; being sane
cannot mean acting as if one were sane.

The theatricality of madness is one clue that alerts us
to the difficulties we have in imagining sanity. Hamlet's
madness makes people suspicious, incites their curiosity,
gets them talking. Even though it is an abstract word,
madness is an abstraction we can visualize, we can picture how it performs. Sanity doesn't quite come to life for
us in the same way: it has no drama. Like the "good"
characters in literature, the sane don't have any memorable lines. They don't seem quite so real to us. Insofar as

we can imagine them at all, they are featureless, bland, unremarkable.

What may seem striking about *Hamlet* to modern eyes and ears is that sanity is not invoked simply as a counter to madness, as a defining alternative. When the word turns up, it is used by Polonius to describe just how impressed he is by the inventiveness, the eloquent intelligence, of Hamlet's supposed madness.

> POLONIUS: (*aside*) Though this be madness, yet there is method in't.—Will you walk out of the air, my lord?
>
> HAMLET: Into my grave?
>
> POLONIUS: Indeed, that's out of the air. (*aside*) How pregnant sometimes his replies are! A happiness that often madness hits on, which reason and sanity could not so prosperously be delivered of.
>
> (II.2.205–11)

Sanity, for Polonius, is a different way of speaking; madness is not worse than sanity, it just makes sanity sound dull. Madness is not opposed to sanity, it has a different method; even though method, of course, is usually associated with reason (even here Hamlet's madness is making Polonius himself more imaginative). Madness hits on things that sanity and reason can conceive of, but not so "prosperously"; Hamlet's madness, though these would not be Polonius's words, is more poetic, more suggestive, more evocative, more flaunting of its verbal gifts and talents than mere sanity. Words can be delivered more or less prosperously; a happiness can be struck by madness that reason and sanity can diminish. Sanity tempers where madness excels. Both are "pregnant," promising the new life that is new words, but they deliver quite differently. It is a difference of quality but not of kind. The words of the mad are more prosperous than the words of the sane; and "prosperous" was then a more prosperous word than it is for us now, as it meant "bringing prosperity; favourable, propitious, auspicious" (*Oxford English Dictionary*). Prosperous words augured well for the future (even though Hamlet's prosperous words didn't, in fact, augur well for his). For Polonius, sanity and madness are two ways of being pregnant with words.

Polonius connects reason and sanity, an association that has become all too familiar to us, and suggests that compared with Hamlet's madness they are lacking in something. It is precisely what sanity may be lacking that Hamlet's madness makes Polonius wonder about (as though the mad expose the sane in the same way that the Fool exposes his Master). The replies of the mad are somehow more pregnant; the dialogue of the sane is poorer. And yet the mad make us suspicious, we can't rely on them to be telling us the truth. Whereas sanity is assumed to be morally good—the folio has "sanctity" for "sanity"—madness may be disreputable; and because it may be, because we can't ever be quite sure what the mad are really up to, it is. The mad don't let us take it for granted that we know where we are with them. Hamlet's madness is artful but duplicitous; Hamlet has good lines but a weak character, at least according to Polonius. Which, of course, immediately raises the question of what more there may be to a person's character than the words they speak. Polonius is so perturbed by Hamlet partly because he is so impressed by him.

THERE ARE equations and conundrums here that we will become familiar with. Madness can be associated with both unconventional truth-telling, and with the intention to mislead. The mad speak in ways we don't understand, but that makes us think that they know something we don't know. They can sound unworldly and unusually intelligent at the same time. And the sane, by the same token, seem more reasonable about their wants, more straightforwardly honest. The mad lack a sense of community, isolated by the pregnant ambiguities of their speech; the sane seem to lack a certain complexity, but live at relative ease in a commonwealth of shared understandings. The sane can, in the fullest sense, get on with people; the mad are difficult.

R. D. Laing was more or less to agree with Polonius that sanity may not be all that it is cracked up to be. The people we are inclined to call mad may be getting at something, may have a way of delivering things, even perhaps of divining things, that the sane shy away from. Indeed, reason and sanity could be a kind of armor, the method in our sanity, as Polonius implies, protecting us from our more pregnant conceptions. If, for R. D. Laing, three hundred and fifty years after Shakespeare wrote *Hamlet*, sanity was seen as a virtual protection racket; if, in the late 1960s the antipsychiatry movement was inspired to intervene in the contemporary treatment of the mad, it was because there is something about sanity as an available norm that oppresses by impoverishing the human spirit. For the antipsychiatrists, the available versions of sanity as a picture of what contemporary people could or should be like didn't do justice to the complexity of people's lives. What was being called madness was, for the antipsychiatrists—and, indeed, for many contemporary artists—simply the return of all the complexities, all the emergencies and nuances in people that so-called sanity (and apparently the psychiatric profession) wanted to exclude. What was being fought over by the antipsychia-

trists was no less than the definition of what human beings were deemed to be. (Modern people's dignity, their
preferred picture of themselves, was at stake.) It was as
though there had been a narrowing of the conception of
identity, and the word for this narrowing—that seemed
to the antipsychiatrists so militant and coercive—was
sanity. It was not, they insisted, normal to be normal.
Indeed, the very things we recognized as signs of
normalcy—reasonableness, even-temperedness, special
concern for others, and so on—were the things that estranged us from ourselves and others. In retrospect,
Hamlet seemed like *Sanity, Madness and the Family*—a key
text of the antipsychiatrists—writ large; and Polonius,
for a moment at least, was the first antipsychiatrist.
What, the antipsychiatrists wondered, was normal
about normal families if they drove people mad?

"Who's there?", the famous first line of *Hamlet*, was
Laing's question too. But Laing had a hundred and fifty
years of psychiatry behind him—the term "Psychiatrie"
was coined at the turn of the eighteenth century by
Johann Reil—which, as it became more mechanistic,
wanted to know what was there rather than who. If people were like machines, subject more to the laws of science than the passions of the heart, the question was,
quite literally, what made them tick? The medical profes-

sion talked about technology, not about the soul; about instincts but not about what made life worth living for people. The radicalism of Laing and his colleagues was an attempt at recovery of what was sometimes, perhaps unfortunately, called "the human" after the depredations of capitalism, which they believed dehumanized us. By "the human" they meant something like a person capable of feeling fully alive. For the antipsychiatrists at their most extreme, sanity meant complicity with everything that was most dehumanizing, most deadening, about culture. Madness was an authentic response to the horrors of contemporary life; to be sane in a world like this was to be out of touch with reality. "We are living in an age," Laing wrote in 1967,

> in which the ground is shifting and the foundations are shaking. . . . In these circumstances we all have reasons to be insecure. When the ultimate basis of our world is in question, we run to different holes in the ground, we scurry into roles, statuses, identities, interpersonal relations. . . . I wish to relate the transcendental experiences that sometimes break through in psychosis, to those experiences of the divine that are the living fount of religion.
>
> *(The Politics of Experience)*

Instead of being a salve for the apocalypse, our contemporary forms of sanity have become, for Laing, the problem. As part and parcel of the forces of secularization our sanity alienates us from divine experience. The "living fount of religion"—a curiously anachronistic Victorian-sounding phrase—is the source of nourishment that madness reconnects us to. Where once people had religious experience to sustain them, now, Laing suggests, psychosis is the closest they can get to any kind of spiritual nourishment. In the wasteland of contemporary life—and there was, even then, something mawkish about Laing's vision—we should look to the mad, to those who are unable to cope, for illumination. The implication of this, of course, was that some people needed to go mad to regain what Laing calls, in a veiled allusion to Hamlet, "true sanity." We are, in Laing's anti–Original Sin view, fundamentally sane creatures alienated into a false sanity by societies we are compelled, against the grain, to adapt to; this false sanity conceals a madness that sometimes—and Laing needed to stress this because there were casualties from his approach, people who hadn't felt restored by going mad—is our lifeline. Madness, at its best, is a journey toward true sanity, toward the authenticity of our real nature; through madness we are in contact with the best things about ourselves. Culture corrupts; madness renews. And what culture corrupts is our true sanity:

> From the alienated starting point of our pseudo-sanity everything is equivocal. Our sanity is not "true" sanity. Their madness is not "true" madness. The madness of our patients is an artefact of the destruction wreaked on them by us, and by them on ourselves. Let no one suppose that we meet "true" madness any more than that we are truly sane. The madness we encounter in "patients" is a gross travesty, a mockery, a grotesque caricature of what the natural healing of that estranged integration we call sanity might be. True sanity entails, in one way or another, the dissolution of the normal ego, that false self competently adjusted to our alien-ated social reality: the emergence of . . . divine power.

What is striking here—apart from the number of words in that Laing needs to make his case—is that it is not only our "divine power" that Laing wants to redeem, but also the word "sanity." "True sanity" as a reunion with divine creative power is the aspiration, the ambition Laing offers us; "pseudo-sanity" is an estranged and es-tranging integration of bits and pieces of compliant but efficient adaptation to a world we are terrified of (false sanity, Laing implies, is like a bag of tricks we have just to

keep ourselves going; we call this bag of tricks "character"). To become truly sane, in this redemptive vision, we
need to dissolve our normalcy. Sanity as a concept has itself been corrupted by a corrupting world; we have been
seduced or tempted by false goods. Sanity is really a sickness of the soul; just as Kierkegaard had said that the
person who was most in despair is not despairing at all,
so Laing wants us to believe that the modern person who
is most "sick" is the person who is not sick at all. Our
lives depend upon getting sanity right; it has come to
mean compliance and submission, social and professional "success"; it should mean being more of a piece
with our "deeper," "truer" inner selves, less estranged
from what really gives our lives value. We should, Laing
insisted, be speaking out, not fitting in. We should be less
well-mannered.

Adaptation, which had been such a good word for
Darwinians, became a dirty word for the antipsychiatrists.
If organisms could survive and reproduce only if they
could adapt sufficiently to their available environments—
if they could use the world they found themselves in to
meet their needs—what was it about the human organism that meant that people could adapt not only at the
cost of their sanity but also at the cost of their lives? Too
many modern people, the antipsychiatrists implied, were
overadaptive; they could survive (and reproduce), para-

doxically, only by betraying themselves. "Sanity today," Laing wrote,

> appears to rest very largely on a capacity to adapt to the external world—the interpersonal world and the realm of human collectivities. As this external human world is almost completely and totally estranged from the inner, any personal direct awareness of the inner world has already grave risks.

What Laing calls "sanity today" is perhaps akin to indoctrination: inner feelings are sacrificed to correct beliefs, and becoming a recognizable member of a group is the overriding aim. He pictures a real person with an inner personal life hidden behind an ideology. Becoming a person means adopting a regime. Thus the "true" sanity Laing promotes is equated with idiosyncrasy, the individual embracing the true grandeur of her eccentricity. True sanity, for him, is singularity, the becoming of who you are, the realizing of a personal vision. And he cites the by now familiar litany of modern artists "shipwrecked," as he puts it, by living in a world that could not bear their inner visions, and who therefore could not bear themselves: Hölderlin, Clare, Rimbaud, Van Gogh, Nietzsche, Artaud. All, in Laing's view, are products and casualties of a viciously censorious world. They are exemplary because they remind us of our "true" sanity (of course, in actuality, most artists don't, and never have, gone mad). True sanity is whatever it is about us that refuses to sacrifice our inner worlds, our singular visions, in order to get on in the outer world, the world as it is. True sanity transforms the world as it is to make room for the unique vision that each individual person contains inside himself. These artists were truly sane because they never sold out; they never tried to make themselves acceptable or winning.

Sanity, for Laing, is an antithetical word; it is used to argue mutually exclusive positions. And this is dramatized by Laing's attempted clarification of the word by presenting it in its supposedly true and false versions. The sane person complies with the world as it is; the sane person has joined the army of the normal. The sane person never complies with the world as he finds it, because compliance betrays the very thing that makes him who he is. What one thinks about sanity depends then on what one thinks about individuality; whether there is such a thing, and, if there is, whether or not it should be privileged. Sanity is used to refer either to what we most value about ourselves, or to what endangers what we most value about ourselves.

But there is an instructive confusion here because madness can be used in exactly the same way: it can refer to what we most treasure about ourselves and to what most horrifies us about ourselves. It is as though these are the issues we are most at odds with ourselves about. Because what is at stake here is precisely how we describe what we most value about ourselves, which includes, of course, the histories of how we have come to our conclusions about these things; our conclusions about what we must—or want ourselves to—be made of. Nonetheless, Laing is remarkable, despite the messianic hyperbole and the conceptual confusion, for wanting to make the case for a desirable sanity.

OUR RETICENCE about sanity—our enthusiasm about madness and our relative carelessness about alternatives to it—is reflected in Samuel Johnson's definitions of the words in the first great English dictionary, his *Dictionary of the English Language* of 1755. Under "Madness" Johnson lists four definitions, with twelve literary examples to support them:

1. Disordered in the mind; broken in the understanding; distracted; delirious without fever.
2. Expressing disorder of mind.
3. Overrun with any violent or unreasonable desire: with "on," "after," or perhaps better "for," before the object of desire.
4. Enraged, furious.

These are passionate definitions about something akin to passion. They stress the overwhelming, the fervent, the disordered, and the sick. Madness is divisive and undermining. Johnson is characteristically impressed by its power, but not by its value (he has his religious faith, his relentless work, his geniality, his civility to counter it with). Under "Sanity" Johnson has in his dictionary merely "Soundness of mind," and gives Polonius's words from *Hamlet* by way of illustration. If it is a word that we have found so little use for but given such importance to—and Laing points this out, even though he needs to sacralize sanity into the bargain—we should wonder what it does for us. Both Johnson and Laing agree that certain states of mind are sounder than others (Johnson gives for "Sane," "Sound: healthy"). But what kind of soundness is sanity? And what kind of soundness of mind is desirable? And, perhaps above all, can we picture the mind as the kind of thing that can be sound?

Sanity, as I have said, has never been a popular word, or indeed (unlike insanity) a condition one might write a book about. No history of sanity has ever been attempted; there are no professional experts on the subject, no famously sane poets. In the Western tradition there are many accounts of the good life, of the religious life, and now, more frequently, of the healthy life; but the sane life has never found its niche in the vast array of self-

improving works that education, whether formal or infor-
mal, has traditionally consisted of. Despite its being part
of the currency of our noblest pastime, self-assessment,
for over five hundred years, there are no revered manuals
we can turn to, no self-help books to advise us on this significant issue. Because its importance, whatever it is supposed to refer to—and even now we are still inclined to
ask, sane from whose point of view, sane for whose
benefit?—would seem to be beyond question. We may be
"poor indeed if we are only sane," as the psychoanalyst
D. W. Winnicott wrote in the 1960s, but we are far poorer
if we are only mad. "Sanity," as a term, has had its uses,
as we shall see; but it has always lived in the shadow of
madness, as the weak antagonist. It has always found it
difficult to match the infernal dramas and melodramas of
madness; our torments have made us more imaginative
than our consolations.

We tend to think of sanity, if we think of it at all, as a
reassuring possibility, almost with nostalgia, as something
that must, by definition, exist as the logical alternative to
madness. Logical and reassuring it may be, but it is also
curiously blank. Yet when we come to define it as a category of behavior, as a way of describing a state of mind
or a kind of person, we are at a loss for words; and the
words we are likely to use about sanity can easily sound
clichéd or ironic. Accounts of sanity are likely to remind

us of the banality of virtue. Sanity, in other words—and there are very few other words for it or about it—has never really had a vocabulary, has never made a name for itself. It clearly exists, but we don't know where to look for it. It is not, for example, something our parents are likely to have told us about. There are no films or novels that are about it, no television programs that have much to do with it. No one is famous for his sanity. It is difficult to picture sanity because we have no pictures of it.

But when we imagine the so-called mad, they appear before us in lurid or horrifying or fascinating or discomforting images. They are the stuff of iconography, the very people other than deities for whom forms of representation seem to have been invented. They have been painted and photographed, described, and diagnosed; they are a shared preoccupation, and a site of conflict for artists and scientists, many of whom are assumed to be mad in order to do what they do. The mad, in the modern era, have written and been written about, have sung and been sung about. Peculiarly and poignantly adept at performing themselves, the mad have been essential to Western drama; tragic, comic, and absurd, the mad cross all genres and disciplines. Madness is all too visible; by definition, perhaps, it makes someone difficult to ignore.

For hundreds of years the mad have had institutions to care for them and to punish them; in their always ambiguous status as ill and/or criminal, they have had experts of a variety of so-called disciplines to treat them, legal systems to contain them, and, increasingly, focus groups to defend their rights. Architects have designed the kinds of buildings they are assumed to need. Pharmaceutical companies and Western governments since the Second World War have invested huge amounts of money in researching the causes and cures of madness; and new professions—most notably psychiatry and psychoanalysis—have been invented for its treatment. The mad, that is to say, mobilize people; they are great motivators. Mental illness as apparently akin, at least in phraseology, to physical illness became in the twentieth century a major social and economic problem. Daunting statistics are regularly produced in the press about the prevalence of depression, schizophrenia, eating disorders, addiction—in 2002, someone committed suicide in Britain every eighty-five minutes, and so on—and yet the sane never receive any publicity. There are, as far as I know, no statistics available about them. The sane are not news.

We know where to find the mad, and who we should talk to about them (psychiatrists, geneticists, neurobiologists, psychoanalysts, chemists, anthropologists, historians, etc.). But where can we go to find the sane? Which buildings do they live in? What do they wear? What are they like and how will we recognize them? Do they have recognizable features, distinguishing marks, common mannerisms? The sane, whoever and wherever they are, have never received the attention or concern they deserve. We have made them up—just as we have made up the whole notion of sanity—but we have never been able, or perhaps willing, to identify them. Like the so-called good characters in fiction, the sane are not vivid to us (and there are, indeed, no characters in fiction or drama who we think of as great sane characters, in the way that there are great mad characters like Lear). It is strangely difficult to describe sanity and to feel that you are adding to the stock of available reality. We can't flesh it out. Our descriptive powers, such as they are, seem to break down around it. We can't even use images from the natural world to represent it (there are mad dogs but not sane dogs; mad hares but not sane hares). Sanity, in this sense, doesn't translate.

We should hear alarm bells when things we claim to value and to want are so difficult to give an account of; when values are too vague they are easy to ignore and to idealize, to promote, but only in ways that mystify. Sanity is too unthreatening to have a stigma attached to it, but its lack of definition, our lack of interest in defining it so that it can be discussed, should give us pause. And if for no other reason than the fact that sanity, when it is mentioned at all, is always touted as an alternative to mad-ness; as an antidote to forms of experience and suffering that we consider to be among the most daunting and pro-found that we are capable of. It is uncanny that a culture so haunted by madness should have a blind spot about sanity. If sanity is a token, an empty verbal device—merely an imaginary foil for what we call madness—then we should acknowledge more openly that "madness" is another word for "human nature." But if we have in-vented the idea of sanity to talk about something essen-tial but elusive about ourselves; if the word is like a dream we have been unable to interpret, or a sign that we can't read, we might be at a loose end without it, lacking some-thing we could really use. The word must be there for a reason.

Sanity promises us something, but we can't quite tell what it is. We can't quite work out how our lives would be better, or even different, if we were sane. Rather like a se-cret society or a lost tribe, most people assume that the sane exist—as standard-bearers, if nothing else, for the possibil-ity that there are people we need not to be frightened of—but can't place them. The sane, even as figures in the mist, are still haunting us, still pressing their staggeringly vague claims. We can't do without them, but we rarely meet them. Unlike the so-called mad—who have made up in drama what they have lacked in intelligibility—the sane don't intimidate us; they don't seem to make their presence felt. Indeed, we are more likely to talk about sane bits of behavior than sane people, as though we think of sanity as something we are capable of, but never defined by. If we are sane at all, we are sane inconsistently.

But to know whether something we want to call sanity is possible at all for us depends upon the ways in which we describe it. And one of the ways it is usually described is as a condition, a state of mind, without quirkiness or intensity; it is associated more with composure and self-possession than with passion and inventiveness; it has more to do with understanding than violence. Sanity, in other words, looks distinctly unprosperous in a culture committed to what it likes to think of as individuality, and flair, and creativity, and enterprise. It may no longer, in this sense, be wise to be sane. It is, perhaps, a sign of our times that sanity sounds so anachronistic, so like something from a counter-culture or a relic we are not quite sure what to do with. Whereas madness is always with us, always our contemporary.

When the mad have not been pathologized as dysfunctional and dangerous, they have traditionally been idealized, if not glamorized, as inspired; as being in touch, as we shall see, with powers and forces and voices from which everyone else is more or less excluded. "The lover, the lunatic and the poet" are famously linked in

A Midsummer Night's Dream, and not only there, because they are all transported and increased by their experience. In these versions of madness, the mad, like lovers and poets, have privileged access to essential truths; they are the heroes and heroines of what they can bear. Scapegoated and idolized as oracles and irritants, as geniuses and fools, as artists and frauds, they are represented as at worst provocative and disturbing, and at best uniquely illuminating. And in the twentieth century numerous reputations have been made in both the humanities and the sciences in an effort to tell us the truth about madness, and about the truths of the mad. The mad have been trailed by commentators, specialists, and supporters. The sane, meanwhile, have been either ignored or caricatured (in Foucault's *Madness and Civilization* (1967), for example, or Laing's *Sanity, Madness and the Family*, the sane are never viewed as complex or as idiosyncratic as the supposedly mad). There is clearly something about sanity that doesn't interest people.

Nor have the sane quite so assuredly been able to identify themselves. Writing about madness, virtually a genre in itself from the late eighteenth century, clearly does not identify one as sane. Though it is assumed in scientific literature that the mad, by and large, are by definition unable to write lucidly about themselves; the implication being that the expert has something that the mad do not have. One definition of the sane would then seem to be, the sane are those who understand madness. And yet sanity is rarely a claim that writers about the mad—or, indeed, anyone else—are keen to make about themselves. Another striking fact about sanity is that it is not something people are keen to own up to, or even boast about. It is as though the sane, by some kind of tacit agreement, are those who would never say that they were sane. They would never use their sanity as the mad might use their madness, to identify themselves. The sane are superstitious about declaring themselves.

And yet, as we shall see, in many of the attempts to sort out the sane from the mad there is a sneaking suspicion that the differences between them may not be quite as convincing as we want them to be. The sane and the mad may have things in common. That the relationship between sanity and madness may be rather like the relationship described by the anthropologist Claude Lévi-Strauss in *Tristes Tropiques* (1955, tr. 1961) between the sacred and the profane. "The opposition between the two terms," he writes, "is neither so absolute nor as continuous as has sometimes been asserted." Whether they are two mutually exclusive categories or different versions of the same thing; whether they are conditions made of words or maps for countries that actually exist, a lot of lives depend on what we use these words to do, and a lot of what we do depends on how we use these words.

The history of sanity is unwritten, and may be literally unwriteable—except, that is, impressionistically, as a history of the uses of the word—because there has never been sufficient consensus about what "sanity" refers to. Unlike madness, sanity has never troubled or fascinated people enough into speculating about it, or classifying it, or specializing in it. There have been no institutions, perhaps surprisingly, to carry a concern for it. Accounts of madness have become more and more sophisticated, more and more contentious over time; but there has always been a failure of nerve or imagination that may itself be a resistance in what became known in the twentieth century as "mental-health professionals" about the whole issue of what it is not to be mad. There are, as I have said, many impressive accounts of how and why things can go wrong for people, and of what we might do in terms of child-rearing, legislation, and political and economic provision to prevent so-called mental illness; but there are far fewer accounts of what a life is like—of what a life should or could be like—when people are not driven mad. What a Good Life is supposed to be like, what a sane life would be, has been the best-kept secret of the mental-health experts. Accounts of good mental health are scarce and usually trivial.

The language of mental health—rather like the language of morality—comes to life, if at all, in descriptions of disability, incompetence, and failure. It is pathology, the breakdown of putative norms of mental health, that gets people going; it is unhappiness that tends to engage people and make them (sometimes) eloquent. But in the language game of mental health, the rules of sanity that are being broken are never properly codified, or even articulated. We are living as if we must know what sanity is because we are so adept at recognizing insanity when we see it. If sanity were a game, how would you learn to play it if the authorities could tell you only when you had broken the rules, but not what the rules were? It would be enough to drive anyone mad. It is as though our common-sense assumption is that if we look after the madness, the sanity will take care of itself. And that because we know what madness is, we must know what sanity is; as though if you knew the color white, you would automatically know what black was.

Unlike most oppositional or related terms, madness and sanity don't function as true contraries; madness is far more emotionally charged—subject to far more official and unofficial description as diagnosis and slang—than sanity. In the theater of language they are an odd couple; they never quite do what they should for each other. As categories, one is too full and one is too empty. Given what significant areas of human experience these words, as the center of a force field, have been recruited to account for—areas of experience essential to our pictures of ourselves, of our histories, of our cultures—this imbalance is of considerable interest. Perhaps we have made sanity unalluring in order to make it unapproachable?

It is as though there is something about sanity that we don't want to go into, that we shy away from. And in this sense sanity is more like a forbidden object of desire: something we are dissuaded from being interested in but can never get away from. And like all forbidden objects of desire—like the man or woman of our dreams—it brings with it the fear that it may not exist, and the wish that it does not exist (after all, if it does exist, what are we going to do with it when we find it?). We tend to downplay sanity's significance, but are somehow attracted to it. Just as we never know whether something is a figment because it is forbidden, or forbidden because it is in fact a figment, we are never quite sure whether sanity is worth bothering with. When we really desire something, or someone, our resistance is likely to take the form of our thinking it too difficult, or not worth the trouble, or impossible. And we work very hard to keep such forbidden objects at a distance, and as unattractive as possible to us. Whether it functions as a norm or an ideal, as a joke or as an achievement, as a gift or a talent, as sacred or profane, sanity tends toward blandness and self-parody. Sanity seems to acquire meaning, to become charged as a term, only when it becomes a negative ideal, when it is scapegoated; when, in order to promote something else—like spontaneity or rebelliousness or passion—it is set up to be attacked. The mad, as ever—though more often, in actuality, their champions and trainers—have all the best lines. Hamlet always kills Polonius, and never lives to tell the tale.

Sanity, in other words, has more often than not been staged as a paradoxical and faintly ridiculous ideal; we may aspire to it, we may, however vaguely, be encouraged to want it; but what we are deemed to want even more is precisely what it excludes. Madness may horrify us, but passion, strange eccentricity, careless and careful transgression—all the ingredients of modern individualism, of life lived to the full—are what fascinate us. Sanity, in this sense, is a representative modern virtue; it bores us, and gives us pleasure only when it is mocked. Sanity may impress us, but it has never been made to seem attractive; sanity may be a good thing, but it is somehow not desirable. The terrifying thing—and it is only the terrifying thing that is ever glamorized—is madness; and, as ever, it is the frightening thing that seems real. Violence in the street is more likely to stay with us, to haunt us—to, as we now say, traumatize us—than, say, the more ordinary kindnesses of everyday life. We may be unaccustomed to valuing things, to exploring things, that are not traumatic. Sanity may be one of these things.

IT CAN SOMETIMES feel as though the whole notion of sanity has been invented as some fictitious vantage point from which the trauma that is madness can be observed. This is because madness as a spectacle, madness as a terror and as a fascination—the sense of being possessed or driven or haunted by something alien and unfamiliar in oneself—has dominated our descriptions of what it is to be a person. We have tended to believe, or have wanted to believe, that there is something inside us—it can be called God or the gods, or the soul, or instincts, or the unconscious, or the ancestors, or the dead, or our histories— that is in excess of our conscious designs for ourselves. And madness, more than sanity, is of a piece with this repertoire of commanding presences under whose aegis, in this picture, we believe that we live. We are part of something not only more powerful than ourselves, but also quite different in kind from ourselves as we imagine ourselves to be. We may be the animals who use language, the animals who can make promises, the animals conscious of our forthcoming deaths. But we are also the animals who have described themselves as subject to a vast array of extraordinary madnesses: depression, anxiety, obsessions, phobias, addictions, paranoias, doubts and suspicions about ourselves and others, feelings of un-reality and insignificance, feelings of grandiosity and cosmic importance. This is the common currency of our lives. We have outdone all other animals in the range of our symptoms. And our relationship to these madnesses—these irrationalities that plague us—has been profoundly ambivalent. People have never been quite sure whether madness refers to the more bizarre forms of malfunctioning, of diseases, that human beings are prone to; or whether, in fact, human beings are intrinsically mad—an exaggeration, perhaps, even potentially a disability, but not essentially alien. Should the project be to attempt to cure ourselves, or to attempt to accept ourselves as we are? Should we, in short, think of our madnesses, our symptoms, as a toolkit we have evolved for dealing with reality, for getting by; or should we think of them as a kind of truancy from our lives, an evasion of what we need to do, a weakness? Are our madnesses an integral and necessary part of our lives, or are they superfluous?

Either nothing that is human is alien—we are what any of us is capable of imagining—or nothing that is human can be alien—we are only whatever makes sense to us. One picture is inclusive, one picture is exclusive; either we are defined by whatever it is about ourselves that we must reject, or we are defined by including everything that we discover about ourselves. But either way the question takes the form: what, if anything, can we or should we do about madness? Should we be including madness in a fuller picture of ourselves, or should we be exorcizing it, where possible, as the saboteur of better lives and better selves? What is it, then, about sanity that makes it so difficult to talk about? It would not be surprising, given the sheer power of our madnesses in their various forms, and the ways in which they are, by definition, beyond our willpower—you can't cure someone of a snake phobia by suggesting that they try to like snakes—that we may be skeptical about the resources we have to set against them. It may be true that we have limited the range of sanity by setting it so starkly against madness. And by underdescribing what it could refer to.

Sanity is clearly a word we use freely so long as we don't have to define it. In the rather one-sided language game of the mental-health professions it is often tacitly assumed that sanity must be everything that madness is not. That we should be able to straightforwardly deduce a picture of sanity from any given picture of madness (tell me what it is for something to go wrong and I can tell you what it is for something to be going right). But if, say, it is mad behavior to be deluded, to see things that are consensually agreed not to be there, is it then sane behavior to see only things that are consensually there? If it is mad to hear voices, what is it then sane to hear? The idea that if you take the madness out the sanity will show through (or vice versa) is rather like saying that because you can drive someone mad, you can drive someone sane; or that because we describe people as going mad, we can describe them as going sane. The two words cannot be so neatly correlated.

SOME MODERN PSYCHOANALYSTS, such as Melanie Klein and her followers, argue that we are born with varying amounts of sanity and madness inside us, and that they, the psychoanalysts, fortunately, can tell these things apart. There are, we will find, two kinds of experts on this subject, as one might expect since this whole question is the secular derivative of the question of Original Sin (Good versus Evil is akin to Sanity versus Madness). There are people, like the Kleinians, who are only too keen to tell us the difference between sanity and madness—that is to say, only too keen to tell us that they already know the difference—and then there are those people, like D. W. Winnicott, who even though they still like using the words (and their associates) prefer to see them as muddled up, to see sanity and madness as subtly interdependent, or indeed versions of each other, on the our-virtues-are-our-vices-and-vice-versa model. For them, implicitly, the distinction between sanity and madness always has a question mark over it.

The first group of Kleinians—most notably W. R. Bion, Hannah Segal, and Donald Meltzer—are averse to madness, though resigned to the inevitability of our unending struggle with it because, like sin, it is assumed to be integral to our nature. The second group—which includes the psychoanalysts Winnicott, Marion Milner, Charles Rycroft, Masud Khan, and occasionally R. D. Laing—think that sanity is good but sometimes overrated, or good for some things but not for others. For them it is good to be sane as a mother, but not good to be sane as an artist. The first group, who unequivocally prefer sanity, have what used to be called a "tragic view" of what used to be called the "human condition." They believe we are doomed by our innate destructiveness; that we are capable of sporadic relief from the madness of our aggression and our subsequent guilt, but that our lives are mostly spent managing this madness. The second group, who have found a way of valuing sanity, are also suspicious of it. They are able to equate it, at its best, with having a realistic apprehension of one's nature—of one's histories, desires, and fears—but at its worst they see it as a cover story for the more compliant and falsely adapted parts of the self. They tend to be more amused than horrified—or full of righteous indignation, traditionally the province of those who think of themselves as on the side of sanity—because they can see how any wholehearted endorsement of sanity, or indeed of any virtue for that matter, tends toward dullness and self-parody. Sanity straight and sanity ironized have become, in other words, the contemporary options. Sanity is either presented as self-evident—it is obviously sane to be kind—and dogmatically promoted or it is valued as something surprisingly equivocal, as a contention rather than a fact—is it obviously sane to be kind to someone who torments you? Sanity is the site where morality is debated, in spite of itself. When people start talking about sanity, they are talking, unavoidably, about what they think we should most value about ourselves. And, of course, what we should do about the less acceptable parts of ourselves.

Sanity has been given other names in the past, such as faith, or reason, or health, or goodness. But unlike these other ideals sanity pits us starkly—sometimes too starkly—against our madness. Sanity invites us to include whatever we have called madness in our moral considerations about ourselves. Sanity reminds us that there is something else we are up against in our desire for self-improvement, in our abiding aspiration for better lives. From the early nineteenth century onward, the notion of sanity has reassured us, presumably because we were beginning to suspect it, that there is more to us than our evident madness, even though that something else has been difficult to identify. As we shall see, by tracing the history and uses of the word, sanity has been nagging away at us for longer than we may realize. And as its history often suggests, sanity often sounds like something only a mad person could have dreamed up.

A WORD FIRST USED in English in our familiar sense of "soundness of mind, mental health" in *Hamlet* in 1602, "sanity" comes into its own from the early nineteenth century onward as the links between so-called mental illness and criminality began to be scientifically studied. It is always a quality of the mind, and not of the body; and its definitions want us to picture forms of harmonious organization, a state in which things are as they should be. So definitions of the word itself, like mild-mannered utopias, tell us something about the wishes the culture reassures itself with. George Crabb's popular *English Synonymes Explained* of 1818 has, under the heading SOUND, SANE, HEALTHY:

SOUND and SANE, in Latin sanus, comes probably from sanguis the blood, because in that lies the seat of health or sickness. . . . Sound is extended in its application to all things that are in the state in which they ought to be, so as to preserve their vitality; thus, animals and vegetables are said to be sound when in the former there is nothing amiss in their breath, and in the latter in their root. By a figurative application, wood and other things may be said to be sound when they are entirely free from any symptom of decay; sane is applicable to human beings in the same sense, but with reference to the mind; a sane person is opposed to one that is insane.

Sanity is to the mind what health is to the body: the state in which one ought to be, which is the state in which one's vitality, one's life force, is preserved. The sane mind works properly, as it should; and so, by implication, there are people who know, people who are able to recognize, the proper workings of the mind. This definition, of course, is not unlike Polonius's definition of true madness, suggesting as it does that a sane mind is one that works sanely. Nevertheless, we get the picture of the mind as an organ, or as an organism, that does at least have a way it ought to be. Although Crabb's analogies, of growing vegetables and healthy animals and undecaying wood, suggest that the whole issue is quite straightforward, in fact, something invisible, the "mind," is being described as akin to something all too visible, like an animal or a plant. This confusion of the social and the organic—assessing the mind and its evidence in human behavior as though it were the same as a body—informs and confounds all the available definitions of sanity. ("If social norms could be perceived as clearly as organic norms," Georges Canguilhem remarks, "men would be mad not to conform to them" [*The Normal and the Pathological,* 1978].) But when sanity is defined in social terms—as a word whose meaning is constructed in its use by consensus—it is difficult to picture.

The *OED* tells us with uncharacteristic vagueness that sanity means: "Health . . . Wholesomeness . . . the condition of being sane: soundness of mind: mental health . . . soundness (of material)." As definitions go—and definitions always go round in a circle in dictionaries, which are always closed circles—"soundness" is perhaps the word that gives us a lead (Skeat's famous *Dictionary of English Etymology* of 1882 has, for "sane," "L. sanus, of sound mind"). Soundness, a contemporary, as it happens, of sanity, and like sanity a representative word of the nineteenth century, is a word that we rarely use now. It comes from a world we have lost.

SOUNDNESS. The quality or state of being sound or free from disease. . . . Firmness, solidity; freedom from weakness, defect or damage; goodness of condition or repair. . . . Orthodoxy in respect of religious belief, political views, or other opinions. . . . The quality or fact of being in harmony with solid or well-established principles, or facts. . . . Thoroughness, completeness.

(OED)

Sanity, according to the solid and well-established principles of the *OED,* is essentially to do with soundness of mind; the mind is assumed to be organic like the body or like a part of the body. Both can be sound and subject to disease. But soundness is to do with a lot of things—like health and orthodoxy and harmony, and solid and well-established principles—that were already in question when the *OED* was first being compiled in the 1850s. These things were clearly more to do with social than organic norms; more to do with consensus and assent and the rhetoric of vested interests. Sanity, and the soundness of mind that is supposed to characterize it, is like a version of pastoral, an idealized state of happy hierarchies and foolproof traditions.

Sanity, according to this network of definitions, is about reliability; it could be another word for trustworthiness, for the demeanor of the successfully acculturated person. It is certainly a word for the intelligible and the orderly; a world of shared values, orthodoxy, and firm foundations. To modern ears there may be echoes of fascism in this—in the images of invulnerability, in the apparent absence of dissidence and anomaly—but the world conjured up by these words is without conflict, a romance of health and harmony and solidity; a world without misfits or intimidation. If this association of sanity and soundness, this belief in the mind and the mind's properties, already sounds old-fashioned in the 1850s, already wistful in its idealism, it is because the words themselves are wanting the very substance and solidity they are asserting. They are like propaganda for a world, a "quality or state of being," that has never existed. Sanity and soundness cannot easily coexist with suspicions about their own soundness. They invite a modern skepticism that they are allergic to, that they are undone by. Definitions of sanity become elegies for a lost world, nostalgic fantasies for a wished-for strength, for an afterlife without struggle and self-division. In a supposedly secular society sanity keeps in circulation pictures of life before the Fall. Of a life, that is to say, in which one's body, and other people—other people's bodies—are no trouble.

As Mr. Meagles in quarantine in Marseilles, in

Dickens's *Little Dorrit* of 1857, says, sanity is extremely precarious:

> That's my grievance. I have had the plague continu-
> ally, ever since I have been here. I am like a sane man
> shut up in a mad house; I can't stand the suspicion of
> the thing. I came here as well as ever I was in my life;
> but to suspect me of the plague is to give me the
> plague. And I have had it, and I have got it.

Why, we might wonder, would it be a problem for a sane man to be shut up in a madhouse? What is sanity if it can't deal with the contagion of madness? There is the implication here that sanity can sustain itself only by staying away from madness; that the only thing that is sane about the sane is that they are the people who keep away from the mad. The sane, Mr. Meagles intimates, are people plagued by suspicions of their own madness. Such life as they have is lived in quarantine. But people are always persecuted by what they protect themselves from. Just as the overprotected child assumes there must be terrifying things out there if he needs so much protec-tion, and can't stop thinking about them, and lives in fear; by the same token, the sane are those obsessed by their own madness.

A recurring theme in the thinking about the history of sanity is an equally recurring suspicion that the mad and the sane may be secret sharers, accomplices in their apparent antagonism, more bound up with each other than either would want to acknowledge. What Mr. Meagles realizes is that the sane man sees something of himself in the mad; that there are connections and affinities—as there are most famously between Dr. Jekyll and Mr. Hyde in Stevenson's story—where we would rather not see them. And our response to their hidden complicity is to try to separate them out; to make the case for their being absolutely different (we make distinctions when we fear the links). And that means to try to produce definitions that make them sound mutually exclusive, in the hope that strict definition will confine them; that, as a kind of word magic, if only we can get our definitions right, there will be no contagion. We will know where we are. But the will to conclusive definition is at best a sign of doubt, and at worst a sign of defeat (Mr. Meagles is nothing if not defeated). The defenses of sanity—the often forlorn attempts to sort it out from madness—are notable for their paucity of definition. We prefer our sanity tacit, without suspicion of the thing.

POLONIUS WAS IMPRESSED, briefly, by Hamlet's madness as a kind of artistry. The essayist Charles Lamb, however, wanted to impress upon his readers that Shakespeare was sane. In an essay entitled "Sanity of True Genius," published in the *New Monthly Magazine* in 1826, he insisted that true genius was synonymous with sanity, not with madness. That an intervention of this sort was required was itself proof that the issue was controversial. If the madness of true genius were to be accepted, then madness would no longer be merely "an illness, a disability," and sanity might seem to be the enemy of art. People who have experience of madness, in themselves or in others—Lamb's sister, whom he nursed throughout her life, was famously mad, having murdered their mother— are more likely to need a viable concept of sanity. Lamb, writing against the grain of what came to be known academically as Romanticism, wanted to promote that most unlikely thing, a proof of the sanity of the greatest artists. The notion of sane art, it is worth noting, has never caught on. "So far from the position holding true," Lamb begins his brief argument,

> that great wit (or genius, in our modern way of speaking), has a necessary alliance with insanity, the greatest wits, on the contrary, will ever be found to be the sanest writers. It is impossible for the mind to conceive of a mad Shakespeare. The greatest wit, by which the poetic talent is here chiefly to be understood, mani-

fests itself in the admirable balance of all the faculties. Madness is the disproportionate straining or excess of any one of them.

The picture Lamb gives, and this will become familiar, is of madness as the disorder of excess. The "faculties" are the kinds of things that can become imbalanced. Balance and proportion are pitted against strain and excess. These so-called faculties may be difficult to imagine, but what is being asserted here, and is exemplified by the true genius, is the idea that what a person is composed of—her humors, her faculties, her predispositions, her instincts—fits together; that we are, at least potentially, harmonious creatures. Sanity presents us with the possibility that we can compose what we are; that madness is an exaggeration, a "disproportionate straining or excess" that we ourselves create, and that we are more than capable of getting the quantities right. But this version of sanity suggests to us that there is something about us—it could be our faculties, or we might call it our desires—that always threatens to elude our grasp. Sanity tends to make a case for itself in the language of measurement and control, even though the language of control is surprisingly vague. "The true poet," Lamb continues,

dreams being awake. He is not possessed by his subject, but has dominion over it. In the groves of Eden
he walks familiar as in his native paths. He ascends the
empyrean heaven, and is not intoxicated. He treads
the burning marl without dismay; he wins his flight
without self-loss through realms of chaos "and old
night" . . . never letting the reins of reason wholly go,
while most he seems to do so.

In this strange vision of composure, of invulnerability, with its allusions to Genesis, to Shakespeare, and to
Milton's *Paradise Lost*, the sane are the unfallen, and the
Fall the fall into madness. It is implied that the mad are
prone to dreaming when they are asleep, to possession, to
a sense of the world as unfamiliar, to intoxication, dismay,
self-loss, unreason. It is a peculiarly contradictory picture:
the sane are Adam and Eve before the Fall—their anti-
type is Milton's Satan—and great geniuses like Shakespeare. Sanity is innocence, guaranteed by a God. But if
there are reins of reason, there is something that needs
reining in. The sanity of True Genius, we must assume, is
that the True Genius is a fallen creature who can write—
who can describe things—from the point of view of the
unfallen.

Sanity, as Lamb personifies it, is a genius for domesticating the fall: "In their inner nature, and the law of their speech and actions, we are at home and upon acquainted ground. The one (the weak writer) turns life into a dream; the other, to the wildest dreams gives the sobrieties of everyday occurrences." The sane genius transforms everything that might disturb us, "the wildest dreams," into something that is familiar and reassuring. It is his artfulness that makes us feel at home; it is the weak writer who makes us feel estranged, or baffled, or lost. True geniuses, like everyone else, as Lamb knows, have their more incontinent dreams at night; and everyday occurrences are not always sober or sobering (and neither, from all accounts, was Lamb himself). The sanity he promotes is a kind of alchemy. The horrifying, the dispiriting, the bizarre are made utterly convivial by the sane True Genius. The unmanageable is transformed by language into the endlessly reassuring, making all disagreeables disappear. It is part of the sanity of Lamb's True Genius to persuade us that there is no catastrophe, no overpowering realm of "chaos 'and old night.'" What Lamb cannot tell us, indeed has nothing to say about, is where "that hidden sanity which still guides the poet in his wildest-seeming aberrations" comes from.

But the other talent of this sane genius is that he—only men are referred to in the essay—is able to seem to be mad, to put madness on, to entertain it. Unlike the truly mad person, he is free to imagine madness because he is not possessed by it. "If, abandoning himself to that severer chaos of a 'human mind untuned,'" Lamb writes,

> he is content awhile to be mad with Lear, or to hate mankind (a sort of madness) with Timon, neither is that madness, nor this misanthropy, so unchecked, but that,—never letting the reins of reason wholly go, while most he seems to do so—he has his better genius still whispering at his ear, with the good servant Kent suggesting saner counsels, or with the honest steward Flavius recommending kindlier resolutions.

What is striking about this—apart from Lamb's association of madness with hatred, and sanity with "kindlier resolutions"—is that Lamb characterizes the sanity of the True Genius as that which tempers the madness, that stops the madness getting the better of him. Sanity checks the madness. Lamb's other key words in this essay are "dominion," "taming," and "subjugation"; as though the sign of sanity is not merely reason, or the absence of madness, it is a talent for controlling madness, for making art out of the madness. It is the madness that makes the sanity so necessary. What comes through most strongly in the essay is Lamb's apprehension, clearly born of first-hand experience, of how unremittingly terrible madness can be. His defense of sanity is a testament to the power of madness.

For Lamb, writing about sanity was the safest way, perhaps the only way, of giving his account of madness. From the protected vantage point of a commitment to a determined belief in both sanity and the sanity of True Genius, he can explore the terrors of madness. The implication of his essay, understated and oblique as it often is, is that only the sanity of True Genius can manage and bear madness. True Genius is literally what is required. We need Shakespeare, we need the verbal gifts of the greatest genius for this task. Nothing, in other words, is rarer than sanity. Madness requires genius to make it viable. Indeed, that may, ultimately, be what genius is, what sanity has to be: a talent for transforming madness into something other than itself, of making terror comforting. Sanity is this talent for not letting whatever frightens us about ourselves destroy our pleasure in life; and this, for Lamb, is essentially a linguistic talent. Shakespeare reclaims through language those areas of experience we are inclined to shy away from. It is Shakespeare's sanity that makes Hamlet's madness so inventive. The creator of a mad character must be sane, otherwise he would be like Hamlet, and could never have written his plays. The sane create, the mad merely suffer.

For Polonius, it was Hamlet's madness that made him so verbally "pregnant." Despite the differences—which we have inherited—the Polonius theory of sanity and the Lamb theory of sanity share an assumption: they both believe that there is something excessive about people, which is called madness, and that sanity sets limits to it. And this, depending on one's point of view, makes sanity a diminishment: of something more "prosperous," in Polonius's view; or of something too severely chaotic and violent, in Lamb's view. Madness tends to be, for the people who use it, the word for this excess in its most unacceptable forms (one of my patients said that she knew she was mad because she "kept brimming over into herself"). Sanity tends to be the word for whatever gets its measure. Madness is equated with loss of control, which is equated with doing forbidden things; sanity, on the contrary, is law-abiding, makes sense, and is equated with self-possession. The preoccupation one could say that they share is, who or what is in charge? Who or what does my life belong to? Sanity, of course, is taken to be the safer state of affairs; madness endangers us, or at the very least it endangers our sanity.

When people speak of their fears of madness, it is often in terms of being invaded or taken over or possessed. People, in other words, divide themselves up into a foreign body, the madness that threatens to take them over, and what must be a sane body (or self) that is the victim. Sanity is rarely described as the colonizer, or, indeed, as in any sense the aggressor. What is at stake, what is being contested when sanity is called up—as Lamb's essay shows—is a life less strange. Our strangeness to ourselves—how easily we can experience our lives as confounding and unsettling—is the point or the problem. Should we be getting used to it as simply our fate, or transforming it into something more familiar? Sanity suggests that we could be at home in the world, living on what Lamb calls "acquainted ground." It is the sanity of the True Genius, Lamb argues, that converts our terror into delight.

SANITY USUALLY EMERGES as something substantive— as a useful and therefore meaningful idea—when it is under threat. It becomes a real thing, a plausible and possible state of mind, when it seems about to disappear. In the horrifying world of Big Brother in George Orwell's *1984,* one of the things that is being fought about and fought for is sanity. In catastrophic situations, like the totalitarian regime of *1984*—and of course in other, nonfictional, regimes—sanity is recovered as a lifeline to something essential. The idea of sanity seems to keep hope alive. "It was not by making yourself heard," Winston the hero-narrator reflects early in the book, "but by staying sane that you carried on the human heritage." The "human heritage" is the good world that has been lost, the world that existed before the regime took over; sanity is the link to this heritage, and the idea of it keeps the heritage alive in Winston's mind. Words like "sane" and "human heritage" are like mnemonics, reminders that other worlds are still possible, that there can be continuity with previous, preferred ways of living. In this critical situation though, it is notable that what is not questioned or considered is what it is or was about that human heritage that preserved sanity.

Winston stays sane, initially, by writing secretly (writers who use the word "sane" often think of writing itself as a conserver of sanity); and sanity involves finding forms of self-expression, despite the Thought Police, who imagine and construct a better, alternative future. And yet there is another face to sanity in the book; or rather there is another version of sanity, which involves quite the opposite—a sanity maintained through ignorance and self-inuring. Indeed, the way people remain sane sustains their oppression:

> The world-view of the Party imposed itself most successfully on people incapable of understanding it. They could be made to accept the most flagrant viola-

tions of reality, because they never fully grasped the enormity of what was demanded of them, and were not sufficiently interested in public events to notice what was happening. By lack of understanding they remained sane. They simply swallowed everything, and what they swallowed did them no harm, because it left no residue behind, just as a grain of corn will pass undigested through the body of a bird.

If sanity depends upon the inability or unwillingness to understand, it is madness to have a realistic sense of what is going on. Or rather—and this is particularly vivid, for example, in the accounts of those who denied what was happening to the Jews in Nazi Germany—it is as though knowing or acknowledging certain things that are going on around you might drive you mad, might destroy your hard-won equilibrium. What is called sanity then becomes a strategy to manage a mad and maddening world. Sanity, in *1984*, is another word for consenting to one's own oppression. The Party relies on the people's capacity for this kind of officially endorsed sanity; but it is this very sanity as a capacity, as a ruse, that courts alienation (it is the way you avoid suffering that makes you suffer). Adaptation means losing the life you think you are protecting. Like R. D. Laing—though Orwell was writing twenty years before Laing—Orwell's narrator equates good or true sanity with individuality. Winston, he writes toward the end of the book, "fell asleep murmuring 'sanity is not statistical,' with the feeling that this remark contained in it a profound wisdom." False sanity is the ignorant uniformity of the Party; any group that demands the pooling of individuality, Orwell believes, drives the individual mad. A sane group is committed, above all, to the individual differences of its members (so in the sane group, paradoxically, there is likely to be more conflict). It is idiosyncracy that the Party condemns. "You are here," the terrifying Party official O'Brien says to Winston,

> because you have failed in humility, in self-discipline. You would not make the act of submission which is the price of sanity. You preferred to be a lunatic, a minority of one. . . . Whatever the Party holds to be truth, *is* truth. It is impossible to see reality except by looking through the eyes of the Party. That is the fact you have got to re-learn, Winston. It needs an act of self-destruction, an effort of the will. You must humble yourself before you can become sane.

Orwell's profound question is, who controls the means of production of sanity? In the chilling and all too contemporary ordeal that is *1984,* it is the very meaning of sanity that is being contested. For both Winston and the Party, sanity refers to, is used to represent, what matters most in life. The Party would say that the best thing about a person is whatever makes him a member of the Party; it is sane to be a member. Winston tries to hold on to the belief that his sanity is his resistance to the Party. Sanity is used by both sides to keep certain—albeit mutually exclusive—values alive. It is a word that neither side can do without to make its case; but, by the same token, as Orwell intimates, it is a fickle word, an unusually powerful rhetorical device. It can easily be recruited to legitimate the most terrible things. Orwell could not have written the book without deploying, and exposing, the language of madness and sanity.

Orwell is warning us that because sanity is such a powerfully evocative term, despite, or even because of, its vagueness, it can be used to legitimate incompatible positions. But that there is something about the idea of sanity that holds our attention is not in doubt for Orwell. If the word "sanity" can be used so promiscuously, so opportunistically, to both manipulate and to reassure—to remind us of our most important values and to exploit our credulity—we need to know how and why it works on us; both what it can be used to do, and the kinds of crimes that can be committed in its name. It is a remarkably shifty word for something that is supposed to inspire trust in us.

However indefinite it may be as a word, however casually we may use it, however lacking in confidence we are about its very existence, sanity carries a big theme. It carries, above all, a hope we have for ourselves, together with our doubts about this hope. Packed up in the concept of sanity is the idea of our lives having a discernible purpose—a "state in which they ought to be, so as to preserve their vitality," in Crabb's words—and of the purpose being the point of living. Whether sanity refers to a realistic apprehension of things as they are or a dream of how they should be, our commitment to the possibility of sanity may be the last enclave of our now age-old belief in progress and redemption; that our lives can be better than they are, and that we are in a position to make them better. The traditional contest between sanity and madness is therefore about the transparency of our intentions, about the extent to which our lives are our own—not subject to the darker forces, the obscurer inclinations—and so can be designed by ourselves for ourselves. What is at stake in sanity is whether we can be at home in the world; whether we are right to think of ourselves as self-fashioning creatures, and whether, if we are not, there is still a way of living available to us that is the right way (when we talk of being "driven," for example, we are assuming that there must be a saner alternative). The right way of living is often described, as we shall see, as closer to nature, or to our nature; and the assumption is that were we closer to the supposed source of ourselves, our lives would be better. It becomes a question, in other words, of whether we are fundamentally sane, but endlessly distracted from this sanity, or essentially mad, and in need of schooling for our madness. Clearly, a lot depends on whether we describe ourselves as born sane and everywhere in the chains of madness, or born mad and everywhere in the chains of sanity. The rhetoric of sanity and madness has to do with nothing less than what used to be called the "meaning of life," and is more likely now to be called, at least by the more secular-minded, the meaninglessness of life.

IF SANITY is a word used infrequently in the arts, it is perhaps less surprising that it is not a keyword in the sciences. Whether there is sanity in the cosmos, in matter, and whether it can be observed and measured has not exactly captured the scientific imagination. Which is why we should take note, if not heart, when sanity turns up in scientific conversations about the purpose, or otherwise, of the so-called universe. "We are children of chaos," the contemporary physicist Peter Atkins writes, and the deep structure of change is decay. At root, there is only corruption and the unstemmable tide of chaos. Gone is purpose; all that is left is direction. This is the bleakness we have to accept as we peer deeply and dispassionately into the heart of the universe

(*The Second Law*, 1986)

It is encouraging, if a little nostalgic, that the universe is deemed to have a heart, but that is the only encouragement to be found here. And yet if there is bleakness, perhaps it is because we have overinvested in purpose and progress. The apocalyptic language, the biblical echoes of "corruption" and "chaos," have all the exhilaration of bad news. And yet the rigorous Darwinian Richard Dawkins, commenting on these bleakly bracing new—though not unsuspected—truths, counsels us against despair. It is simply the "very proper purging of saccharine false purpose," he writes, with the familiar tough-mindedness of the fully converted:

Such laudable tough-mindedness in the debunking of cosmic sentimentality must not be confused with a loss of personal hope. Presumably there is indeed no purpose in the ultimate fate of the cosmos, but do any of us really tie our life's hopes to the ultimate fate of the cosmos anyway? Of course we don't; not if we are sane. Our lives are ruled by all sorts of closer, warmer, human ambitions and perceptions.

(*Unweaving the Rainbow,* 1998)

Dawkins is presuming here that we do tie our life's hopes to our sanity, and that sanity resides in what we do tie our life's hope to. Of course if we are among the majority of people in the world who live in theocracies, the ultimate fate of the cosmos is key. But whether or not most people in the world are insane, sanity could rightly be said to depend on what we tie our life's hopes to; what is sane for Dawkins is a life ruled by something other than those particular rules of the cosmos (it is as if, in a sense, he is telling us that in order to be sane we shouldn't worry about what the world is really like). It would be insane to pin one's hopes on the fate of the universe, apparently, because the universe is an unstemmable tide of chaos, corruption is the order of the day. Both Dawkins and Atkins are wondering, as well they might, what it would be like to be sane in the world discovered by modern physics. Dawkins proposes that we should, in a proper purging and debunking, acknowledge the scientific facts of life; but then to be or to stay sane we should tie our hopes to something cosier. Sanity here depends upon what you can ignore, the facts that you can stop yourself feeling. It is sane to keep meaninglessness at bay.

Dawkins wants more immediate, more personal hopes as a haven in a heartless world, and equates sanity with what it is realistic to hope for. But the implication is clear: if we were to pin our hopes on the cosmos, as described by modern physics, it could drive us mad. If the universe is decay, corruption, and chaos, then our (more hopeful) sanity must be our belief in growth, purity, and order. Sanity is being presented here as a stay against chaos and entropy; as though the sane self is not driven mad by the meaninglessness, the carelessness of the cosmos. In such a bizarre and uncanny world, sanity is our lifeline. What Dawkins doesn't consider is why we need a sense of purpose, of meaning, of growth and progress, to feel that our lives are worth living. It might, as we shall see, be sane now to live in a way that makes our preoccupation with such age-old ideals disappear.

Just like the sanity of Lamb's True Genius almost two hundred years ago, the sanity of Dawkins's scientifically enlightened modern person resides in whatever it is we can do that prevents us from succumbing to chaos. Sanity staves off dissipation (and it does, clinically, tend to be the case that people who are committed to, or overimpressed by, their own sanity tend to have acute intimations of emotional chaos). The sane part of ourselves gives us the right hopes, the ones that keep us going. We assume, in other words, that it must, by definition, be sane to believe that life is worth living, or at the very least that it is sane to want to believe this.

Sanity is usually appealed to in calamitous times. Under political oppression, or in the light of the more daunting scientific discoveries, people are encouraged to keep their head while all around them others may be losing theirs. Or sanity is asserted by its promoters as a value to reassure us that the times are not as calamitous as we think they are ("no sane person could possibly . . ."). Its use, then, tends to be an index of our fear; indeed, using the word at all is often a way of calling for help. When sanity is referred to, or called for, something is usually about to disappear, as though the word is always a portent of a great loss in the offing (Polonius's recognition of Hamlet's sanity heralds the attempt to get rid of Hamlet; no one after Charles Lamb will write about the sanity of True Genius). If it begins to occur to us that perhaps the mad use language more prosperously than the sane; or that the great art that we value most is the product of madness; or that the political and economic realities we have consented to are the problem and not the solution to our suffering; or indeed that the cosmos revealed to us by our prize possession, science, undermines all the hopes we have traditionally had for ourselves, so that our cultures and our physical universe—even the verbal language that distinguishes us from the other animals—are maddening, then sanity becomes the great good place. Sanity becomes the fantasy that keeps us sane; a rhetorical prop in an unplotted, threatening world.

When the historian G. M. Trevelyan praised the poet Meredith in 1908 as "the poet of common sense, the inspired prophet of sanity," it was clearly an elegy for common sense, if not a nostalgia for inspired prophecy. Inspired prophets of sanity, as we shall see, have been few and far between; partly because sanity has more often than not been described as at odds with inspiration, but also because sanity has been used to persuade us that there is such a thing as good common sense; and that we would all be better off if we abided by it. We should be more surprised than we are that the prophets of sanity are so rare and that there is so little agreement about who they might be.

What we refer to as common sense is a kind of taken-for-granted sanity of everyday life; as though there is something inside us that we all share, and that were we to follow it sanity would prevail. And yet for many people today, common sense—and the whole notion of an ordinary and available sanity that is bound up with it—is extremely elusive. Common sense is increasingly something we can no longer agree about. Indeed, what, if anything, we have in common with each other, and what we can do to keep ourselves sufficiently sane, have become our abiding contemporary preoccupations. Whether multiculturalism is compatible with social cohesion; whether we can guarantee our security only by sacrificing our freedoms: these are our political considerations now. On the world stage it is not the sanity of politicians that we are most struck by.

Like a phantom limb or a prosthetic device, sanity is something to conjure with. Once the notion began to catch on in the nineteenth century, once it became handy, it was never let go of; it was used casually, but it was never looked into or analyzed. It is worth asking now, before it dissolves in its own vagueness and banality, what sanity as a conceptual tool, as a keyword, actually means. We will have to ask, whenever sanity is invoked, what is it being used to transform or to conceal, what is the conflict it is being used to resolve? When we are told, in any given situation, that sanity has finally been restored, we need to know what the people in that situation think has happened. If it makes us feel sane to believe that Shakespeare was sane, or that the cosmos is not, we need to know why.

PART two

Making the Case

I. A Mad Start

"Now the mind is called sane," Erasmus wrote in *The Praise of Folly* (1509), "as long as it properly controls the bodily organs." Though written nearly five hundred years ago in a tract defending Christianity, this sentence more or less formulates our modern assumptions about sanity. First, that sanity is a quality of the mind, not of the body (we don't describe people's bodies as sane or insane). Second, that it is the function of the sane mind to control the body, and therefore that the body would be out of control—or at least doing forbidden things—if it were not under the aegis of the mind. Third, that the body is not only the kind of object that can be controlled, but also the kind of object that can be controlled properly or improperly; so what the sane mind understands above all, is propriety. And last, but not least, there is a time factor involved. For sanity you need a mind, and you need a mind to control an otherwise insane body, but the mind is called sane, as Erasmus says, only "so long" as it controls the bodily organs. The implication is that sanity is precarious, not a permanent condition. The question becomes not merely whether the sane mind can control the body, but for how long.

The creatures that we most familiarly think of as having only intermittent control over their bodies are infants and children, as well as the ill, the old, and the criminal. But in Erasmus's terms, which we have inherited and virtually taken for granted, we are literally born insane. Or, to put it a little less starkly, babies have many of the qualities associated with madness—incontinence, inability to work, and inadequate (indeed, absent) verbal skills. They require continual surveillance or they might damage themselves, and by damaging themselves, they damage others; and they seem to live the excessively wishful lives of those who assume that they are the only person in the world. That we are born without what we call bodily control, without language and without regard for others has, as many people have noticed, serious implications. Babies may be sweet, babies may be beautiful, babies may be adored, but they have all the characteristics that are identified as mad when they are found too brazenly in adults. We don't call babies mad, because we believe, insofar as we are able, that they are entitled to do as they can't help doing (though many men, and some women, treat babies as though they were insane); but we don't tend to think of babies as sane either. It is only when they fail to do what we call "develop" that we begin to wonder. Sanity as proper control of bodily organs—including the organ we speak with, the mouth—becomes, however tacitly, the aim of development (we expect children to become continent and articulate as soon as possible). What there is to grow out of is something akin to an original madness; what there is to acquire is the sanity to manage this madness. The most striking, as well as the most daunting, thing about infants is the immediacy of their bodily needs; they are urgent bodies seeking successful—that is, gratifying—expression of their wants. Sanity might in this context mean simply being able to use the mind, the imagination, to both elaborate and to defer one's gratification. Sanity here is creative patience; or a talent for making patience creative. Sanity is a necessary good in the struggle for development, that is, the struggle to survive and reproduce.

Sanity tends to be the word we use for any preferred state of mind. It is what we all think we desire. Like madness though, sanity is not exactly a technical term, part of the jargon of a specialist discipline. It is often simply respectable slang for something important to do with what is now called "mental health." "We are poor indeed if we are only sane," the psychoanalyst (and pediatrician) D. W. Winnicott wrote; and for most of us, at least when it is quoted out of context, this probably conjures up some encouragement, some quasi-official permission to be as eccentric, as noncompliant, as idiosyncratic as we sometimes feel ourselves to be, or indeed wish that we could be. But when Winnicott wrote this, we should remember, he was writing about young minds, and about something about young minds that we may be eager to forget. In a footnote to a paper of 1945 entitled "Primitive Emotional Development," Winnicott wrote: "Through artistic expression we can hope to keep in touch with our primitive selves whence the most intense feelings and even fearfully acute sensations derive, and we are poor indeed if we are only sane." This is blithely put, and not the kind of thing psychoanalysts—or indeed anyone else—were likely to be saying after a war in which there had been so much destructive "primitive" feeling. But by now it sounds like a familiar point; and a rather exhilarating picture of what art might be, and be able to do for us. Winnicott's suggestion was relegated to a footnote, though, because it is rather more disturbing, rather more startling in its assumptions and its implications, than it sounds. Winnicott is saying not that children are mad, but that what adults feel is mad, is normal for the child. Our earliest lives are lived in a state of sane madness—of intense feelings and fearfully acute sensations. We grow up to protect ourselves from these feelings; and then as adults we call this defense "sanity." Looked at this way, sanity begins to sound like a word we might use for all adult states of mind in which we are not children, in which we do not experience things intensely. We are poor indeed though if this is our only idea of sanity.

For Winnicott, the question was not, what can we do to enable children to be sane, but what can we do, if anything, to enable adults to sustain the sane madness of their young minds? The paragraph that Winnicott could not include his famous footnote in—perhaps because it disturbed him—is as follows:

It is sometimes assumed that in health the individual is always integrated, as well as living in his own body, and able to feel that the world is real. There is, however, much sanity that has a symptomatic quality, being charged with fear or denial of madness, fear or denial of the innate capacity of every human being to become unintegrated, depersonalized, and to feel that the world is unreal. Sufficient lack of sleep produces these conditions in anyone.

By "unintegrated" Winnicott means not minding being in bits and pieces; and believing that from time to time you will, as he puts it, "come together and feel . . . something." This is the so-called normal infant's normal state. In other words, what we call sanity might mean being deprived, or depriving oneself, of the ordinary infantile and childhood experiences of not being, as we say, "together." Sanity would then be the intolerance, in the adult, of madness, unintegration, depersonalization, unreality (tiredness), and so on. The child's true sanity, one might say, resides in his access to, the availability of, or his unprotectedness from these states. And these particular states of mind are, in Winnicott's view, a fundamental resource that the adult wards off, calling this warding off sanity. It is the capacity to be disturbed by our feelings—something that can happen to us in the making and the experiencing of artworks—and to be nourished and sustained by this disturbance that Winnicott is promoting. Our sanity can be the way we sever our connections to the feelings and experiences that matter most to us. The sanity we seek out as a refuge from fear can also be a way of starving ourselves. Winnicott is encouraging us to take on our own turbulence.

Children, for Winnicott, are mad in the best sense of the word, while adults become sane in the worst sense of the word. Referring to himself, Winnicott once wrote in a review of Jung's *Memories, Dreams, Reflections* (1965), "I was sane, and through analysis and self-analysis I achieved some measure of insanity." Development here means the recovery of the insanity of childhood; but perhaps only a measure of that madness is ever possible. Sanity, Winnicott intimates, is a necessity, but it is never enough. If sanity is invoked as a cure for the intensities of childhood, the question becomes, how sane can we afford to be? The paradox of development is that we aim for a sanity that itself becomes the problem.

This is an unfamiliar version of a familiar story. From the late eighteenth century onward, many artists and writers seemed to retell the biblical story of the Fall. In Rousseau, in Blake, in Wordsworth—among many others, and Freud would take his equivocal place in this tradition—there is a new fall, the fall into adulthood. Or more exactly, the fall out of childhood. To grow up into adulthood, to grow up into civic society, was for these writers a journey away from the source of whatever was most valuable about ourselves; whether the child was a "little philosopher" or a "primitive," he was above all vital, full of energy, passionate. What we now call "development" began to be talked of in terms of losses as much as gains, in terms of compromises, betrayals, and disillusionments as much as in terms of achievement, mastery, and sophistication. It was not so much that the child was innocent, and that growing up corrupted her; it was that the child felt intensely, and that growing up diminished her. When Rousseau announced that men were born free and were everywhere in chains, he was introducing us to the idealization of childhood. The child had something—call it a passionate nature; but to become an acceptable member of society he had to sacrifice this nature for something supposedly better. Blake called these two predicaments Innocence and Experience; Freud Civilization and its Discontents; and Winnicott "Sanity" and "Madness."

By the twentieth century, science replaced theology in such debates; the new currency became genes, nature, and nurture. But there remained a fundamental belief that young minds were the minds that most mattered, and everything started in childhood. Childhood might not be an exact predictor of later experience, but without childhood there could be no later experience. Likewise there could be debates about what infants and children were really like; contesting stories could be told about what children were—whether bundles of instinct, bundles of genes, or bundles of cognitive predispositions—but what was no longer in doubt, and it is easy to forget that this is a relatively recent phenomenon, was the privileged position of childhood. Whether or not people went on believing in gods of various kinds, virtually everyone went on believing in the power of origins; that where we get to depends on where we start from.

And yet what modern accounts of childhood development from Benjamin Spock to John Bowlby tend to stress is the child's dependence: what the child lacks, and therefore what he needs to acquire to make his life viable. In the first instance the child tends to be described in terms of what he is unable to do for himself; in terms, that is, of what he requires adults for. And there is, of course, a consensus that the aim of child-rearing—however various the descriptions of the child's development are—is not to drive the child, or indeed the parent, mad. All prescriptions for child-rearing are, albeit tacitly, projects to produce the sane child. That is to say, very few of the modern theories of child development take the child's sanity for granted. The idealization of childhood, the pastoral myths of parenting, are complicit in their denial of the child's emotional turbulence.

In one picture, the art of growing up—the art of growing up sane—involves fashioning one's original madness into sufficiently acceptable forms; and sufficiently acceptable forms mean, simply, ways of living that sustain one's appetite for life. In the alternative picture of development, sanity is more like an overcoming, a mastery, a disciplining of the mad desirings of childhood. In the first picture, sanity is a way of being acceptably mad; in the other, it would be the defining achievement of sanity—or of its stablemate, maturity—that it would bear as little resemblance as possible to the childlike. It is a question, in other words, of whether we view development as a prolonging of childhood, or as a superseding of it. Are adults people who are even better at being children than children are? Or are they precisely the opposite; are they, in fact, those who are able to relinquish the pleasures of childhood? What exactly is supposed to develop in development?

If infants and children are mad in Winnicott's sense—"primitive selves" constituted by "the most intense feelings and . . . fearfully acute sensations"—then there is an obvious sense in which sanity could be seen as a form of impoverishment: an abjuring of passion. If we are mad in childhood, as Erasmus suggests—in improper control of our bodies—then sanity becomes a necessary achievement. The pleasure of mastery replaces the pleasure of gratification; or rather, gratification becomes the mastery of appetite, the pride of self-overcoming.

For both Erasmus and Winnicott, writing as they do out of the Judeo-Christian tradition, it is the body that is the problem; and both seem to have a similar picture of what sanity might entail (the denial, the refusal, the tempering of appetite). They both implicitly link madness and appetite, but the place of appetite, the significance and meaning of desire—with childhood representing the nakedness of desire—is quite different in each account. In Erasmus's redemptive Christian myth the body has to be somehow transcended; in Winnicott's Darwin-and-

Freud myth there is no life but the life of the body (Winnicott defines fantasy, as Freud might have defined art, as "the imaginative elaboration of physical function"). Sanity begins to look like, at worst, the illusion that we can take flight from our bodies; and at best it seems to describe the ways we have of distancing ourselves from the immediacy of appetite. It is as if the sane part of ourselves believes that appetite is a kind of insanity, a strange thing for an animal to believe. Children are not born sane. Babies don't believe in their appetites, they are their appetites.

Appetite and fear are inextricably connected; and all creatures are endangered by the fundamental project of meeting their needs. But the human creature meets his needs, in both senses; unlike every other animal. He must meet his needs in order to survive, and over time he will have to become acquainted, too, with what he will learn to call his needs. And what he will meet, unlike any other animal, is the exorbitance, the hubris of his appetites. Indeed, the stories he will be told about his appetite—explicitly in words, and implicitly in the way his appetite is responded to by other people—is that it is, at least potentially, way in excess of any object's capacity to satisfy. He will be told, in short, that he is by nature greedy. He will discover, whether or not this is quite his experience, that he apparently always wants more than he can have;

that his appetite, the lifeline that is his nature, that is at once so intimate and so obscure to him, can in the end drive him mad. He may be sane, but his appetite is not. This is what it is to be a human being: to be, at least at the outset, too demanding.

Satisfactions are of course possible, but disappointment and disillusionment are unavoidable. At best one can develop a bearable sense of one's limitations and of life's limitations; at worst one is driven mad. Given one's appetite—given the ways we have inherited of describing it—one becomes realistic, or one lives in the no-man's land of the tantrum and the grudge. To talk about appetite, in other words, is to talk about whatever it is that we have to complain about.

In the Original Sin tradition, secularized as the Original Greed tradition, the child is born with more aggression than he can bear. This aggression, which is variously called Hate, Destructiveness, or Envy—and sometimes, more reassuringly, is deemed to be a kind of birthright of vitality—is assumed to be either innate (a product of our genes, with each person having a different amount) or provoked by excessive frustration (and again with each individual having a different tolerance of frustration). This innate aggression—when it is not described as living a life of its own, as a kind of "mad" internal saboteur—is always in the service of appetite. There is the straightforward vigorousness of hunger, and there is the rage of frustration, of having to wait or of being left unsatisfied. As the mother can never be in the child's total control, there is always a gap, a delay between desiring and satisfaction. It is in that gap that what is called the madness— the overintense feelings—turns up, when the waiting becomes unbearable and starts turning into something else (the rage and resentment that are the hatred of appetite: the blankness and anesthesia that are the abolition of appetite).

Madness is a word for too much aggression, or too much frustration, or both. Sanity, as a consequence, is either a matter of luck—one happens to be born with just the right amount of aggression—or it is the capacity to bear frustration. The capacity to bear frustration, like religious faith, is the belief—without flight into bitterness or arrogance—that the good thing, the thing one wants, will come. This version of sanity is usually called hope. The sane person can pursue and wait for what she wants without needing either to disparage her desire for it, or disparage the it that she wants. In a sane state of mind one doesn't want to spoil any of the ingredients of one's appetite; neither one's bodily nature that is its source, nor the process and project of wanting, nor the object of desire itself.

It may be madness to hate wanting, but what, if anything, makes it possible for a person to love wanting, or at least to like it enough? In terms of a child's development this raises a question about how we describe that child, about what we observe and imagine and construe to be going on inside the child as she grows from absolute dependence to relative independence, from total involvement with others to a virtual solitude of her own. And indeed about what we take it that the people looking after her can do for her. The traditional philosophical question of whether virtue can be taught becomes a question about whether sanity can be taught. The contemporary child is described as either insanely desirous—loving and hating excessively (and "excessively" here means in excess of some putative adult norm of passionate life); or as insanely chaotic—unable as yet (through immaturity and/or insufficient parenting) to organize and control his feelings (and "feelings" here mean subjective reactions to internal and external pressures; and these reactions, it is often assumed, are the kinds of things that can be more or less organized). The modern child; too much desire; too little organization. But this, of course, is the child seen from the point of view of adult aspiration. This is not how the child describes herself. This is how, in talking about the child, the adults talk about their fear of their own madness.

Once the child ceases to be an emblem of innocence,

he becomes an emblem of madness. This madness, on the one hand, can be idealized as a passionate, elemental energy and wisdom; or, on the other hand, the modern child can be described, with some trepidation, as a seething cauldron of untamed sexual and aggressive instincts. (One prominent British psychoanalyst, Neville Symington, has compared having a baby with the dropping of a bomb into a family.)

Our modern and often realistic terrors about children's vulnerability, about the terrible things that can be done to children, also mask our own terrors about what children can do to us. Childhood, however insistently we try to make it nice—or make it fascinating, which is our other version of pastoral—is a modern word for the insanity of the human condition. The ways in which we conceive of children, our obsession with child development and with so-called parenting skills—the religion of contemporary middle-class child-rearing—has become a code for our forlorn attempt to find a sanity for ourselves. If children are not, in our terms, actually mad, they have been burdened with the fears adults harbor for their own sanity. All the modern prescriptive child-rearing literature is about how not to drive someone (the child) mad, and how not to be driven mad (by the child). Children would be very surprised, I think, to discover just how mad we think they are.

And yet one of the messages we are given by writers as diverse as Wordsworth and Freud, as Blake and Dickens—and Winnicott's account of what he calls "primitive selves" is perhaps the most compelling contemporary example of this—is that while infants and children may be mad, it is this very madness, these "most intense feelings and . . . fearfully acute sensations," that are our life force. Without this first madness, without being able to sustain this emotional lifeline to our childhoods—to our most passionate selves—our lives can begin to feel futile. Winnicott's word for this is "poverty." (In a similar vein the French psychoanalyst Jacques Lacan describes what he calls desire as "that without which our lives feel null and void.") The sanity we aspire to in socializing, in making acceptable the mad feeling and wanting of our earliest lives, can itself be the problem. Sanity, at its best, becomes a sustained and sustaining madness. And above all it depends on—and is made possible only by—the ways in which the adult world responds to the infant's original intensities. The optimism of this view is in its assumption that the child's so-called madness is manageable by adults; it is not intrinsically unbearable, it is only as unbearable as the surrounding adults make it. And, it is presumed in this view, if we are not excessively at odds with the people who look after us—if there is sufficient understanding, or at least sufficient willingness, to make sympathetic sense between parents and children—then we need not be excessively at odds with ourselves. Nothing about a child, assuming she is neurologically sound, is beyond the capacities of the human community. This, one might say, is the good-enough-fit theory of child-rearing. The child will be okay as long as his parents are; and by the same token, any of us might have been okay if only we had the right parents. There is sanity, but perhaps not for us.

But in the bad-fit theory of child-rearing, things are not so promising. The child is not only utterly dependent on his parents, he is also utterly dependent on his nature. Right at the outset his desire is (or may be) too exorbitant for anyone, including himself, to really bear; and/or he may be born in a chaos of urgent and emergent feeling. "How is it," the Kleinian psychoanalyst Roger Money-Kyrle has asked, "that any part of the mind ever becomes sane?":

Eder [one of the first British psychoanalysts] is reported to have said: "We are born mad, develop a conscience and become unhappy; then we die." If this is a despondent view of life, the first part of it seems to me to be indubitably true. Whether the infant mind is wholly unintegrated at birth, or disintegrates at the shock of birth, no one can doubt that the newborn infant is in a state of chaos. And the chaos easily becomes a persecution. Sanity, then, is not something we are born with, but, in varying degrees, painfully acquire. . . . But the sane world never wholly absorbs the chaotic one. Perhaps it is never more than a firm island of sanity in a sea of chaos which continues to exist unconsciously. Meanwhile, the chaotic part, which has not been tamed by contact with reality . . . appears to undergo its own macabre development. . . . At any rate, concurrently with the development of a sane self in a sane world, I think there is always, in varying degrees, the development of a mad self in a mad world of its own creation.

Moreover the insane part is experienced as a terrifying enemy, whose aim it is to rob the sane part of its sanity and take its place.

("ON THE FEAR OF INSANITY,"

In *Collected Papers of Roger Money-Kyrle*, 1978)

This is, of course, an extreme view; but it is a picture, I suspect, that is shared, more or less knowingly, by many people. It is certainly not difficult for many of us, as inheritors of Judeo-Christian morality, to see the struggle between the sane and the insane parts of the mind as a secular redescription of the battle between the forces of

Good and Evil. Clearly, in this picture, emphatic as it is, there is nothing to be said for the mad world; it is chaotic and deluded, and therefore persecutory. Once again, order, classification, and judgment are deemed to be sane. Sanity is what culture can, to some extent—"never more than a firm island of sanity in a sea of chaos"—bring to the innate madness of the human being. And culture, the child's upbringing, as it is called, is about tempering the madness of fantasy. We are born insane fantasists who have to learn to temper fantasy with reality. Sanity is the realism required for psychic survival. So, we might ask, what has to happen for contact with reality to do the necessary taming that is sanity?

Original Chaos could be deemed to be on the one hand something akin to the "blooming buzzing confusion" of so-called mental life that the American psychologist and philosopher William James described. In this view the infant as a rudimentary person is a bundle of inchoate, unstructured feelings, assaulted intermittently by need, and requiring protection from an always potentially overstimulating external environment. On the other hand, there is something like a chaos-creating instinct in the child called "destructiveness," the "terrifying enemy" of Money-Kyrle's description. This destructiveness, this innate hatred, is supposed to attack everything in the infant's world that loves and nurtures him. In this latter, more traditional picture the child is more or less doomed—his destiny is cast—by the amount of destructiveness he is born with; and the onus is on the people who look after him to mitigate, as far as they can, his destructiveness (through understanding, through firm resistance, and through punishment). In this ersatz Christianity, sanity equals love, which equals growth and development, the restoring and protecting of the good thing; sanity is what once would have been called kindness. Insanity is the hatred that for some reason—and the reason is difficult to discern—hates life. For this model to be tenable there have to be people who are able to speak on behalf of Life, who can tell the difference between a destructive and a creative act. Only then can they know what it is about the child that should be fostered, and where the disapproval and dismay should be aimed. But the forces of cruelty and disarray, as Money-Kyrle makes abundantly clear—and one only has to watch the news to begin to feel that there might be some truth in this version—are always in the ascendant. Whatever is sane about us adds up to mere fragments shored against our ruin. If, for Winnicott, sanity is something of a cover-up, for the Original Chaos theorists sanity is our only hope for survival. The child has to be rescued from the madness he is heir to. Parents have every reason to be frantic as they try to avoid adding to the sum of the world's natural insanity.

The modern child, one might say, wants too much; either more or something quite other than what is actually there. As a demonic fantasist the child has to be redeemed by acknowledging reality. The word for this acknowledgment is sanity. If the child is too ruinously aggressive; too selfish, envious, or jealous; a dark destroyer, the child has to be redeemed by becoming a nicer person. The word for this niceness is once again sanity. Or the child has to make do with whatever his nature happens to be; sanity also becomes the word for not betraying one's desire, for not sacrificing whatever it is that makes one's life livable; for carrying through, for transforming and elaborating the desires of childhood. In this antiredemptive myth of growing up in which childhood is not sacrificed for adulthood—in which sacrifice is not the organizing metaphor—there is a growing into oneself. The word for this ruthlessness once again is "sanity." In each of these scenarios, or morality plays, it is insane to live a life that destroys, or spoils, the best things in that life.

The whole notion of sanity may be an attempt to medicalize morality—to speak of the good in the language of health: to make us more accurate, more scientific in our wanting—but by the same token it becomes a form of moral blackmail. It is as if to say: if these are not valued—if these forms of wanting and feeling and speaking and doing—are not cultivated and encouraged and rewarded in the child, then the child will be mad. Or the parents will be driven mad by the child. If the child is not saved from his childhood in these particular ways, then where once he would have been punished, now he could remain insane, meaning doomed to the worst kind of unhappiness that is available to people. Modern Western childhood has never recovered from, or been recovered from, the redemptive myths of Christianity. To be sane is to be saved.

All these myths of development and growth and transformation are ways of dealing with the basic fact that life doesn't work, at least not in the way we want it to work. Child-rearing is the ever-renewed attempt to make a life work. And so it is perhaps not surprising that our myths about the time span of a life tend to err on the side of what we call, usually without irony, the pessimistic (we are only pessimistic, presumably, because we expect to get what we want in the end). That life is not what we expect it to be, that reality is not of a piece with our anticipation, is what we need the (sane) child to know. And yet we want the (sane) child to go on wanting because his survival depends upon it. Wanting is always a species of prediction; development is about finding one's way with,

and through, unpredictability. The idea of sanity high-
lights and muffles this contradiction; the word is used
when the hope that wanting always is—the hope that one
can imagine and find whatever it is that one's development requires—clashes with whatever makes wanting so
very different. It is sane for the child—and, as we shall
see, for the adult—to go on wanting while being able to
acknowledge and deal with the conflicts that wanting always involves.

If childhood initiates us into the rigors and delights of
desiring—of living through appetite, and therefore living
through cooperation with the people we depend on—the
sexuality that begins in adolescence is the new wave of
this urgent wanting that organizes our lives. The sane infant may be hard to find in the stories we tell about growing up, partly because we are prone to describe our
appetites as more akin to madness (when we talk about
eating now we are likely to talk about eating disorders). It
is not surprising then that sane sex, as we shall see in the
next chapter, can seem like a contradiction in terms.

II. Sane Sex

STRUNG OUT BETWEEN romance and pornography it is no longer clear what men and women want to use each other for. And though the disturbance between the sexes—more evident than ever in the media images of carefree happiness and undistressed bodies—is written and spoken about everywhere, there are still very few useful, memorable words about sexuality. The excess of words and images, whether specialist and academic, salacious or moralistic, and the myriad ways in which they fail to haunt or inform or inspire us, suggest that sexuality is now openly spoken of but everywhere repressed.

When people speak about sexuality they become banal, repetitive, and narrow-minded; as though sexuality were a kind of a drug or a dogma or a popular religion requiring no more than a few images and ten truths to keep it going; as though we use sex now to get rid of sexuality. It is as if sex is not something we really enjoy, but something we want to free ourselves from. The sheer strain of keeping sexual desire alive, and the sheer strain of finding ways of satisfying it; the amount of work that goes into making desire desirable; the despair and confusion that many people feel about their so-called sexual lives; the proliferating sexualities available now and the death of the idea of sexual liberation. All these contemporary factors conspire to make people wonder about the place and the significance sexuality should have in their lives. What would it be now to have a sane attitude toward sexuality—both one's own and other people's—instead of taking flight into cynical or exhilarating platitudes about the madness of love or the perversity of sexual desire?

At once alien and intimate, one's sexual desire as it begins to emerge at puberty can seem like the most personal, the most idiosyncratic, thing about oneself; the fingerprint of one's most passionate ambitions and prized affections. The lives of adolescents are driven and defined by crazes and crushes, by intense loves and contemptuous hatreds. But their sexuality, their passions, can also be experienced as something akin to a possession, as something that can lead them into temptation despite their moral principles. As though there was something about themselves—something like a force or an energy inside them—that had little regard for their more sensible beliefs and assumptions about how they should behave. As adults they will discover that sexuality can be something so tenacious that people will risk their lives, their reputations, and their livelihoods in their quest for satis-factions that often don't make sense to them. And that many of the things that they are being encouraged to be-lieve in as they grow up—through education, through re-ligious instruction—are ways of regulating their sexuality. There is something that is irresistible that apparently needs to be resisted. We may feel driven, but we must be driven by the right things; and sexuality as a, or even *the*, driving force has traditionally been viewed with consider-able suspicion.

It is often acknowledged that the best lives, just like the worst lives, are driven lives. On the one hand, we ide-alize the artist, the lover, the person with a passion for jus-tice, the person who seems to have no choice but to do the good thing that she devotes her life to; and on the other hand, we fear the addict, the workaholic, the per-son who is driven to ruin his life, to harm himself and others. It is the project of the cultures we grow up in to tell us what our lives should be driven by, what we should have an appetite for, what forms our passions should take. A sane life in this context is either one in which a person is driven by the right, by the socially acceptable things; or it is a way of describing a life in which one is not driven at all. But either way sanity tends to suggest an unusual de-gree of self-possession, of independence in relation to appetite. Whether the sane person resists his hungers, or has found satisfying ways of including them, of weaving them into the texture of his life, his sanity will be a story about appetite.

In Judeo-Christian cultures the sane person—the sane part of the person—would be the antagonist of what would have been called sinfulness; sanity would be pitted against all those bodily desires that distracted the individual from his duty to God. In secular cultures sanity has a more puzzling role to play. It is obvious why a divinely created creature would want to be good; it is less obvious why a modern, instinct-driven, accidentally evolved creature should want to be sane. Unless, of course, what we are calling sanity is actually a bridge between two worlds, between the wish to be good—to be without sin—and the wish to survive and reproduce. Sanity as an issue, in other words, turns up at the point at which people are beginning to wonder whether virtue and emotional survival are still compatible. And nowhere is virtue put into question more than in our erotic lives.

All the new thinking, like all the old thinking, agrees that there is something catastrophic about being a person. The catastrophe is located in various places: in our being born at all, in our being condemned to death; in our vulnerability as organisms, or in our cruel injustices as political animals; in the scarcity of our natural resources, or in our greedy depredation of them; in our Fall, or in our hubris. But all these catastrophes, one way or another, are linked to our appetites, as creatures who want, and who are driven by, what is at once necessary and missing from our lives. Our wants may be "constructed"—given form by the language available in the culture—but that we want is not in doubt. It is whether our wanting has catastrophe built into it—whether our wanting is such that ruinous frustration or ruinous aggression is inevitable; or is indeed a necessity to keep wanting on the go—or whether our wanting is made unbearable only by the ways in which it is responded to, that is now in question. The language of sanity and madness provides a vocabulary for asking and answering questions about appetite.

Appetite, of course, covers a multitude of activities, if not a multitude of sins. And sexuality is the most confounding of appetites because it is not sufficiently like hunger, the one appetite that seems to make sense. Human sexuality, even though it is an animal sexuality, is not at all like the sexuality of other animals; it is not geared exclusively to reproduction, and it does not have a natural rhythm or periodicity to it.

Human sexuality, instead of being preprogrammed like the instincts of other animals, seems to be fashioned from the tension between the individual's genetically inherited biological potential and the cultural forms she is born into and can make for herself. Unlike the sexuality of other organisms, human sexuality is surprisingly, and sometimes shockingly, diverse in the forms it can take; and because it is a human sexuality it is invested with a range of symbolic significances: a sexually active person in this culture is taken to be, depending on one's point of view, more fully alive, more emotionally deprived, more honest, more healthy, more sacrilegious, more hostile, and so on. Indeed, what is understood to be sexual—or what might be sexual about children, parenting, happiness, madness—is itself subject to varying and contentious interpretation. What is taken to be sexual, and what the implications are of something being of sexual significance, is always uncertain despite the ways in which sex is common currency. Instead of asking whether everything (or just some things) is sexual, we should be asking, more pragmatically, how would our lives be better—more interesting, more amusing, more exciting— if we describe them as sexual? The mere fact that we can describe our sexuality, that we can find sex where we might not expect to, or indeed want to, makes human sexuality the exception rather than the rule.

Clearly there is nothing we would describe as sane or mad—rather than, say, surprising or unusual—about the sexuality of other animals. And we don't tend to classify the wonders of nature in terms of mental or moral health. But when it comes to human sexuality, description is always morally fraught; one way or another judgment is always being passed and assumptions being made, including assumptions about just what it is to be human. We may wonder what we are deemed to be when we are no longer human; and dehumanization, interestingly, is a key word in the classification of sexual practices. It is dehumanizing to treat people sexually in ways that they have not consented to. And we prefer to think that people who relish such things must be mad, as though the word itself legitimates our distaste. By freeing us to disapprove it protects us from whatever else we may be feeling. In this language, which is of course a relatively recent way of talking about sexuality, it could never be sane to dehumanize another person; so sanity becomes the guardian of our preferred version of ourselves. The inflicting and the suffering of too much pain or too much pleasure—with or without consent—are both essentially dehumanizing acts. In ordinary language sane sex is never too aggressive, and it is love that humanizes the sexual act.

The whole notion of sanity, closely allied as it is with stories about love and kindness, gives us guidelines to appropriate sexual behavior, even if the appropriate and the sexual are often uneasy bedfellows. But it is sexuality as destructive—of development, of well-being, of love, of consent, of the law, and of the body—that has always been the issue. A pastoral idea of love is often there to stop us from thinking about the perverse nature of human sexuality. Love reassures us, or reminds us, that sexuality is not only the doing of damage; or that the damage people do to each other in so-called sexual relations can itself be sustaining. The aggressive element in the sexuality of other mammals is evident; but it is sadomasochism that differentiates what is human about human sexuality. The sexual pleasure in inflicting and enduring pain—the scale of imaginative invention that has gone into the sustaining of sexual excitement through tricks and techniques of dehumanization, of treating the other person as an object, not a subject—is one of the defining characteristics of human sexuality (torture is far more imaginative than erotic life). If human sexuality is often enough dehumanizing, we may need to reconsider our ideas about the human. If human sexual excitement so often requires the infliction or the suffering of pain, we may need to reconsider our ideas about sexual excitement. If, as the psychoanalyst Robert Stoller writes, "the need to dehumanize, which has its origins in traumatic, conflict-laden childhood experiences, is built up from hostility" (*Perversion:The Erotic Form of Hatred,* 1975), and childhood is always, in varying degrees, traumatic and conflict-laden, then revenge may be one form that sexual excitement is likely to take. Simply because we have been children, our sexuality is going to be an uneasy mix of the imperious and the servile; and any account of our sexuality that attempts to obscure this will be misleading.

"The hostility in perversion," Stoller writes, "takes form in a fantasy of revenge hidden in the actions that make up the perversion and serves to convert childhood trauma to adult triumph." All adult sexuality has perverse elements in it because every childhood is traumatic; and every childhood is traumatic because every child experiences intense primitive feelings, combined with an absolute dependence on the parents. Without parents or other kinds of caretakers, a child is resourceless, the barest victim of his need and his environment. Through revenge fantasy, and the enactment of revenge fantasies with an accomplice, the adult who was once that child secures himself again; reinstates a lost safety in the form of a triumph. He needs to dominate where he was once dominated. It might be sane not to need such triumphs, but it would not be sane to repeat the terrors of helplessness (except, perhaps, in the safety of a sadomasochistic ritual).

The inevitable trauma of childhood—that can be mitigated but never abolished by parents—is the immediacy of desire ineluctably combined with the bond and the bondage of dependence. The trauma of adolescence, which is itself a recycling of childhood, is the surge of sexuality and the newfound capacity to actually do what one has only as a child fantasized about (i.e., killing the parents, having various forms of sexual access to them). There is now the bodily competence to murder and conceive, to bully and to submit in far more dangerous and subtle and exciting ways, to love and hate more voraciously. The adolescent—and the adults around him—often experience him, perhaps unsurprisingly, as rather mad. Indeed, a sane adolescent would have something wrong with her.

ADOLESCENCE IS a period of transition and transgression. Desiring the parents, the forbidden pleasure of childhood, is replaced by not desiring the parents, the forbidden pleasure of adulthood. Depending on the parents as the primary source of well-being is gradually given up as one becomes both more self-reliant and more or less able to entrust oneself to people outside the family. Sexual desire is the route out of the family, as the adolescent realizes that what she now wants so keenly she cannot get from parents or siblings. It is manifestly a process of separation, but it is experienced as a slow murder, a protracted killing-off. It means that sexual excitement is always linked with a kind of ruthlessness; the parents were the original source of one's pleasure, now one's pleasure depends upon their exclusion. The violence, and the violation of pleasure-seeking, is brought home to one; or one must do everything one can to avoid pleasure seeking. The adolescent begins to take on the full consequences of desiring, one of them being that he can never predict the consequences. In taking his chances, in following through, in keeping faith with the coincidence of one's desire and an object of one's desire—of something or someone happening to turn up and our being reminded that there was something we wanted—there is a guilty freedom. If it is sane to abide by the rules, if there is a familiar well-being about being good (even though we often describe our sexual desire as a desire for the forbidden), then sex becomes a form of madness. This is the double-bind that the adolescent is initiated into: it is good to be law-abiding, but if you abide by the law, you will never get what you really want. It is sane to sacrifice your desire for your duty, to sacrifice wanting for being wanted.

All our stories about the madness of love are stories of impossible conflict; not merely of people trying to make choices between competing options—between, say, the family and the beloved, like Romeo and Juliet—but of choice suddenly seeming to be the wrong word. We go on doing something that we call making right and wrong choices and then we find ourselves in a situation in which choice doesn't apply. Tragedy, in which people are traditionally driven mad, is also the name we have given to those situations in which people find they have to come up with something else to do as well as make choices. They have to acknowledge the limits of their willpower. Like the child for whom it could never quite make sense to have to choose between his parents—even if that is what he is also having to do a lot of the time—the tragic hero is finding out where choice applies. It is integral to our picture of sanity that the sane person is able to make choices; just as it is integral to our picture of the lover that nothing plays havoc with rational decision making more than sex. The adolescent, in other words, is being trained—encouraged, educated, and manipulated—to be a sane, sexually desiring adult. But the sane bit is about choice making, and the sex bit is about the impossibility of choice making. Coming to terms with this would be enough to drive anyone mad.

Why is it that human sexuality is so disturbing and disturbed? How has it come about that we have described our (Western) sexuality as ineluctably linked with madness, and have aspired nevertheless to become sane creatures? How have we—and why have we—made something so essential so alien, in our fashioning of so self-hating a myth?

It is strange that "sane sexuality" sounds like a contradiction in terms; especially since we don't tend to describe the sexuality of other animals as insane. We are never surprised that we are fascinated by the madness of love, by the excesses of other people's sexual lives, as though there is something about our sexuality—its essential madness—that it is impossible not to know; even if we would prefer to acknowledge it only in other people. If modern adolescents experience their emerging sexual desire as a kind of inner terrorism—and adults often experience adolescents as terrorists, as secret agents full of furtive, disruptive, and potentially violent plans—it is because this is the way sexuality is transmitted to them both directly and indirectly by the adult world.

"Madness," Joseph Conrad writes in *The Secret Agent* (1907), his novel about revolutionary terrorism, "alone is truly terrifying, inasmuch as you cannot placate it by threats, persuasion, or bribes." It may be reassuring for us to believe that there is something about us that can be untouched by culture—by placation, threats, persuasion, and bribes; the sexuality that turns up in adolescence again after the first passions of childhood, and is everyone's brush with madness. We need the idea of sanity to help us to believe that upbringing and education are worthwhile, that culture works, that whatever is sane about us can be placated. Sanity is part of that peculiarly modern vocabulary of hope that depends on progress; on the belief that what makes our lives worth living is that they can be improved. Adolescence has to be something that one recovers from; but like childhood, or middle age, it is also something to be grown out of.

If we take the tragic heroes Oedipus, Antigone, and Narcissus as our founding mothers and fathers, as among the lead characters in our sexual myths, even though none of these fictional characters is known for their soundness of mind, we can formulate two propositions about human sexuality. First, parents and children seem to want more from each other than is good for them. And second, that individuals want more from themselves than is good for them. Because modern Westerners are born into and grow up in situations in which they want too much from each other, so-called development becomes a project of wanting too much from oneself. The notorious insanity of excessive interdependence called incest turns into the insanity of excessive self-reliance called narcissism. As animals, human beings must feel uniquely deprived if they want so much from each other and then grudgingly end up asking for so little.

There is a disparity in our erotic lives between what we want and what we actually get, and between what we assume we want and what we actually want. Sexuality plays havoc with our logic, with our just-so cause-and-effect stories, with our modern obsession with security in human relations, and with our ability to make promises. In short, our sexuality seems to make us unreliable to ourselves and others, and it is sexual desire that is the something about ourselves that makes us untrustworthy, uncivil. It is this that has made our sexuality mad, bad, and dangerous to know. Our erotic lives uncover the fact that our preferences do not necessarily accord with our standards. Our preferences (what we long for and crave) and our standards (the kinds of creatures we would rather be) usually have a sadomasochistic relationship of taunting and teasing and punishing (think how difficult it often is to justify our sexual desires to ourselves). What we want and what we should want has become an endless drama of mutual humiliation. Our sadistic relish in exposing the privacy and so-called hypocrisy of others—as much in the tabloid press as in the "revelations" of contemporary biography—is clearly one of our privileged contemporary sexual pleasures.

Despite our wishes to the contrary, children are not born into a pastoral world of human relations. What the child receives as enigmatic and always puzzling messages about his parents' sexual relationship—the mime-show of family life—the adolescent begins to uncover and reenact.

Every adolescent is living through the biologically programmed resurgence of sexual hunger fashioned by his childhood experience. Every adolescent inherits, in more or less obscure forms, their parents' sexual preoccupations—their beliefs and assumptions and fantasies about what people can and want to do together. Their parents' relationship is inside them, like DNA, continuing to work itself out; entwined with their own relationships with their parents and siblings. Though most of this is going on outside conscious awareness, the adolescent, not surprisingly, seems unusually self-preoccupied; and the adults around him, not surprisingly, want to keep him busy with, if possible, improving activities. It is not uncommon for parents of adolescents, like parents of the very young, to feel that they are being driven mad by their children. Nor indeed for them to fear for their children's sanity. When parents say, as they very often do, that they are at the end of their tether, they are describing the feeling of being released into something horrifying; against which, of course, they need tethering. At puberty, when sexuality truly takes over, what adults most fear in their children is madness, pregnancy, and suicide. If none of these things happens in the maelstrom of adolescence, sanity will have prevailed.

But what is it about adolescence, apart from the new-found physical competence to carry it out, that makes suicide such an issue? And that by the same token makes us equate sanity with the belief that life is worth living? It is part of the "madness" of adolescents that adults usually cannot bear, to really wonder whether life is worth its difficulties. The survivors don't want to be reminded of their doubts. The adolescent discovers something that, in a sense, he has always known, but that he has been encouraged as a child to forget and to disbelieve, to refuse to consent to; and this is, that he has little control over his moods. And one of his moods, one of his most gripping preoccupations, will be a sense that life is impossible, that life doesn't work; or that it doesn't work in the way he has been taught that many other things work (like nature, like machines, like wishful daydreams); that life is too painful, too pleasurable, too full of conflict, too confusing; that it is—and he is right about this—beyond him. Like alcoholics who require everyone to drink, the adults in his life will do everything they can to get him to join in, to cheer up, to see the point (this, broadly speaking, is what both parenting and culture are for: luring people into seeing the point). It is one of the characteristics of the people we call insane that they do not have sufficient regard for life. Adolescence—one of the greatest sociological inventions of the postwar period—is the first time the individual has the passion and the intelligence available to consider what life is worth to him.

It is not incidental to this issue, to our terrors about it, that what would be called, academically, the "history of suicide" is not taught in schools. And yet the most cursory reading of this history is instructive. It is telling—how could it not be?—even in its most potted form. "The idea that killing oneself is both a sin and a crime," Arthur Droge and James Tabor write in their appropriately entitled *A Noble Death* (1992),

is a relatively late Christian development, taking its impetus from Augustine's polemics against the "self-destructive mania" of the Donatists in the late fourth and early fifth centuries and acquiring the status of canon law in a series of church councils during the sixth century. Throughout antiquity, the act of taking one's life had been respected, admired, and even on occasion sought after as a means of attaining immortality. Now it became the focus of intense Christian opposition. It is a profound irony of Western history that later Christian theologians condemned the act of voluntary death as a sin for which Christ's similar act could not atone. . . .

That suicide should be a taboo subject [tells] us something about the thoughts we must fear. Both the psychological and sociological explanations of suicide can be seen as a form of "medicalization," for both operate on the pathological distinction between the normal and the abnormal. Both attempt to explain the cause of disease not as an individual choice but [as

a drive—] something over which the individual has little control. In medical discourse it is psychic derange-
ment that compels an individual to suicide; in
sociological discourse, it is . . . social [dislocation].
Both wrest control of the act of suicide away from the
individual, denying the suicide agency. From [this]
perspective, suicide is . . . a "symptom" of both individual psychopathology and social disorganization,
[rather than] a religious and moral problem.

Where once there was sin—and, indeed, heroic
virtue for the non-Christian—now there is symptom. De-
rangement, essentially possession or loss of control, replaces moral consideration as the language of choice. If
it is mad to commit suicide, then the notion of sanity becomes a term of propaganda; Big Brother says it is sane
to want to live. The notion of sanity is there to stop us
from thinking. There could be a version of sanity,
presumably—which would not be absurd to adolescents
or others who subscribe to it—that would be able to include the possibility that life may not be worth living
(with or without the promise of immortality); that could
incorporate the idea that there may be a part of ourselves
that finds life unbearable; that life is something we are
weighing up and not merely taking for granted, and that
this in itself needs to be neither a guilty pleasure nor a

shameful secret. For the adolescent—for whom nobility, and what we would call self-worth, is always an issue—sexuality embroils her in the question of life against death. For this to be treated as a form of madness; for this to be experienced by adults as deranging, tells us something about the precariousness, about the anxious complacency, of the forms of adulthood we have evolved. It tells us how the rhetoric of sanity can be used as a kind of word-magic to wish away the urgent preoccupations—beginning in childhood and continued in adolescence—that are our life-line; but are our lifeline only if the deathline is kept open.

Like any addiction, our addiction to being alive is an attempt to narrow the albeit overwhelming complexity of our minds. Part of the project of adolescence is finding out what makes adults so addicted to life. So addicted, in fact, that they go on with that hopeful, that most fantastic form of pleasure seeking called sexuality. Is sex, modern adolescents wonder, a good-enough cause; and if not, what, if anything, is?

The big problem about sex, the adolescent discovers, is that it is so pleasurable. And this pleasure is initially re-vealed in masturbation. If in Christianity masturbation has been a sin, second only to suicide, it is because sinful-ness was the only way of acknowledging, of being free to describe, our most urgently forbidden pleasures. What is transgressive about both acts is what might be called their selfishness, the ruthlessness of their satisfactions. In both acts what is dispensed with is the need for other people, either permanently or temporarily. It is this violence, and the violent truthfulness that they may contain, that has made both suicide and masturbation into such shameful, such absurdly horrifying acts. The self-engrossed individual for whom the future is irrelevant—except that most immediate of futures, the moment of release—is our negative ideal; is, in fact, our description of the madman. Perhaps it is our profound solitariness that is our most forbidden pleasure?

The key question for the adolescent is: what connections can be made, or are worth making, between his or her masturbatory fantasy—romantic or pornographic— and sexual relations with another person? Is masturbatory fantasy the route to other people—a kind of trial action in thought—or a way of insulating one's desire from others? Is it a refuge, or a way into the world? Sane sex, at its most minimal, may be a form of sociability; it is desire as a medium of contact. The adolescent is urged— sometimes by her desire, mostly by the desires of others— to make what is most private and singular, acceptably public and suitably shareable.

Yet what isolates the adolescent—and bonds her in groups of similarly isolated adolescents—is the turbulence and perplexity of her feelings. There could be no

Good Mood Guide for the adolescent because what he is discovering is that he cannot will himself into preferred states of mind. His moods lead a life of their own that is often at odds with the life he is being encouraged to want, by himself and by others. There may be a voice inside him urging him to be kind, but that voice itself may not be kind; it may be intent on depriving him of the risk that is desire. There may be a voice inside him urging him to be cruel, but that voice itself may not be cruel—simply fearful of tenderness, or the longing for intimacy. And there will be, informing all this volatile, shape-shifting emotional life, what he will learn to call sex. But the word itself will be a necessary oversimplification; a way of referring to something that goes on between people, which draws them toward and away from each other. Something so brimming with fantasy that actual sexual acts can seem, to the adolescent, like afterthoughts, too real to be experiences because so much of sex has been prepared in fantasy.

The homework of sex that is fantasy evolves out of childhood; and childhood is an awkward training for the rigors of adult sexuality. The passions of childhood turn up in the adolescent saturated with the anxieties and inhibitions and power relations that were the self-cures and compromises required by growing up. If in this mêlée, in this fraught history that everyone brings to fruition (or otherwise) in puberty, there can be some notion of sane sex, it would have to refer to forms of sexuality that were not overly harmful. For the adolescent this question phrases itself as: is there such a thing as harmless sex? And if harmless sex is a contradiction in terms—if there is no sexual excitement without an aggressive intention, no sexual exchange without unpredictable and therefore disturbing consequences—erotic life is above all about damage limitation; about getting away with pleasure seeking, and also getting away from it. In masturbation, in the self-pleasuring of daydream, the adolescent suffers the pains and pleasures he prefers; and the damage seems to remain under control.

The principal legacy of childhood that the adolescent has to work on, and to work with—complicated and implicated as it always is by the unique particularity of his personal history—can be simply stated. First, that sexuality always includes a potential for harm; and second, that what is desired is forbidden. Adolescents both fear and desire pregnancy, promiscuity, drug taking, aggressive confrontation, rule breaking, ideals, and adulthood. The prohibited, the dangerous, and the reassuring are the parameters of their world. When the child begins turning into an adult, this feels more like an eruption than an evolution. So-called development seems to have a newfound uncertainty attached to it. And this uncertainty, as ever, is linked to excess. Adolescents are always immoderate.

The way we experience and describe adolescence today may tell us more about our assumptions about adulthood—about normalcy, about sanity, about how we like to think, rather nostalgically, about the life cycle—than about the adolescent in her own right. If the adolescent has become our figure for a kind of normal insanity, for a stage, like infancy, in which the individual is expected and therefore allowed to be incontinent and excessive in lifestyle, then we must take adulthood to be an overcoming, a coming to terms with, or even (in old-fashioned language) a disciplining of a developmentally appropriate insanity. We don't, in other words, take our sanity for granted; we just prefer to locate our natural insanity at two discrete points: in the transition to childhood that we call infancy, and in the transition to adulthood that we call adolescence (with menopause and midlife crises tacked on later). And, of course, at each of these transitions passion and appetite are at stake. There is the normal insanity of people behaving appropriately badly at what we tend to think of as biologically programmed periods of significant change. Then what we call sanity conjures up a recovered stability—the infancy or adolescence or midlife crisis that goes on too long is quickly diagnosed—and keeps us in the picture of manageable change; change with a beginning, a middle, and an end. We may have preprogrammed holidays from our natural stability, but if everything goes according to plan, sanity can be achieved or recovered. One of our innate assumptions is that change is always crisis; our lives are not in a state of continuous revolution, but they are punctuated by dramatic events. Sanity keeps alive the idea of stability as a normal condition; but it also refers to whatever it is about ourselves that can weather change and transform it into new forms of reliability. The reason that sane sex seems such an impossibility is because our sexuality is always potentially at odds with this cherished reliability that we supposedly seek while working so hard to disrupt.

Sanity is on the side of continuity partly because all our madnesses are about rupture (madness, by definition, is isolating). The sexuality that erupts at puberty threatens to rupture the adolescent's connection to the parents. For the adolescent the desire that kept him in the family, and that kept him alive and growing in the family, now leads him out of the family. The lure now is other, unfamiliar bodies, the undomesticated experiences of risk and solitude. And in this formative transition—in which his sexuality is so obscurely of a piece with his past: in which he translates himself out of family life, out of being someone he easily recognizes and can take for granted—

he will develop an obsession. Whatever his history, whatever his hobbies or habits or talents or interests, he will become obsessed by rules. His life will be organized, more or less knowingly, around propriety and defiance; it will be about what can be declared, and what needs to remain furtive. However timid or brash he is by nature, he will be intent on discovering what is authoritative about the authorities, what the difference is between a taboo and a protection racket. He will, as any parent will tell you, drive his parents mad. Or rather, he will try to drive them mad to find out what, if anything, their sanity is made of.

IT IS NO NEWS that desire is transgressive and that pleasures are usually stolen. It isn't startling that we are fascinated by people who break the law, and impressed by people who can do extraordinary and original things by sticking to the rules. But it is difficult to take seriously, or perhaps just to know how to take, our abiding ambivalence about rules, whatever they may be. Most of the ways we describe people, and all of the ways we judge and diagnose people, involve an account of the kind of relationship they have with the rules. Our founding myths—of Oedipus, of Narcissus, of Prometheus, of Antigone, of the Fall—like our tabloid newspapers, are all about people breaking the rules, or the more official rules that are called the law, that are reputed to hold the known world together; and about what we and they think about this. The marriage of scandal and righteous indignation, of outrage and punishment, are the staples of all human drama. The context is always that of crime and punishment; of people wanting to be good or bad, or good and bad, and of people being punished (by gods or fate or the world), and wanting to punish and be punished. Ancient myths and biblical stories are about taboos; novels are about adultery; songs are about betrayal. As a theme the drama of rules is remarkably resilient.

Madness is often associated with the breaking of taboos, whether as cause or consequence (either you have to be mad to break a taboo, or madness is akin to the punishment of breaking one). And, by the same token, sanity is often bound up with a capacity and a willingness to abide by the law. This means, of course, knowing what the rules are, and what a rule actually is—which might involve knowing how a rule came about, what problem it was there to serve and solve, what the reasons are that justify it, and what the consequences are of disregarding it. It might also entail being able to follow a rule, having the requisite capacities to do so. Any culture that uses the word equates sanity either straightforwardly, as in Orwell's *1984*, with obedience; or more minimally, with the acknowledgment that there are rules and that they work in certain ways, whether or not one chooses to abide by them. These are the issues, never formulated as such, that the adolescent is initiated into at puberty. As a child she is likely, as we say, to have learned the rules; whether they have made any kind of sense to her, or any sense worth having, is another matter. As an adolescent with her new-found strengths, and the newfound vulnerabilities they bring in their wake, she becomes for the first time preoc-cupied by the rules because she senses herself to be a po-tentially serious lawbreaker. This is when the rules become an obsession; it's not merely that the stakes are higher, but that the stakes are suddenly as high as they can possibly be. She can really do the things that the un-protected can do. And this, perhaps inevitably, leaves the adolescent with one persisting question: can you follow a rule—follow in the sense of comprehend and abide by—without trying to break it? You don't know whether the law is worth having if you don't risk yourself in the face of it. You don't know whether you are worth having if you don't or can't put the law at risk.

Adolescence is a crisis—a madness one could say—because the adolescent is trying to work out whether life is worth living. Sexuality—in its preferred version as love—is traditionally conceived to be a form of madness because it always confronts us with a seemingly banal question, but a question that starts most startlingly in adolescence; is it worth the trouble, is the pleasure worth the pain? For the sane, it is implied such questions are no longer an issue. They have been answered before they have been asked.

If the adult world is inclined to say better sane than sorry, the adolescent is likely to see the adults as being in an all too sorry state. Whether one wants to be one of the nice and good, or whether one wants to feel rather more excitedly alive is an acute dilemma for most adolescents (and not only for them, of course). The compatibility, or otherwise, of such ambitions—the extent to which it is possible to follow one's desire and to go on admiring oneself—has to do with one's relationship to the rules and, of course, to the people who break them. We allow adolescents a moratorium on their sanity only on the understanding that it will come to an end. It is clearly not sane to go on, beyond a certain point, testing the rules to see if they are made of anything (magic, consent, words, divinity, and so on). Sex and so-called sanity, as most adolescents discover, don't go well together because sexual excitement, whatever else it is, is always about the breaking of rules. Sane sex is a contradiction in terms, because the penumbra of our associations to the word "sane" conjure up—as a kind of tacit knowledge everywhere consented to but nowhere agreed upon—a dignified apprehension of limits. At sex we are not dignified; and our limits can never be taken for granted.

IF SOME KIND of sanity is something we want but secretly do not desire in our erotic lives, it is because sanity keeps us in the realm of the already known. Living within our means, living with a realistic sense of our limitations, is at odds with our experience of sexual desire. The love stories that have taught us how to love (such as *Romeo and Juliet*) are more about risk than complacency, about the ways in which desire takes people out of themselves and into a new life that feels like more life than any they have ever had before. The sanity lost in the madness of love is the sanity of knowing who one is. Only a culture that believes people could and should know themselves would have a use for the idea of sanity, because sanity is nothing if not the capacity and talent for self-recognition. But how does the self-knowing self recognize anything new about the self? To know one's limits is to limit oneself to the self that one knows. So, sanity also always describes the familiarity we have with ourselves that we use for protection against catastrophic change. If it is part of our sanity to know ourselves, we have to ensure that what we know keeps us sane.

It is nowhere more evident than in our erotic lives

that only our most selective attention can keep us sane, can keep us where we are already. Our aliveness, our excitement about life, is thus depleted by the need never to endanger ourselves. Ideas about progress or development may be the ways we have bribed ourselves to believe and have confidence in change; yet our ideas of sanity spell at once an acknowledgment and a wariness of just how catastrophic change can be. At their most extreme our fantasies about sanity become our refuge from the new; or rather, from the new as the too disturbing.

" 'IT IS THROUGH MADNESS that the greatest good things have come to Greece,' Plato said, in concert with all ancient mankind. Let us go a step further," Nietzsche writes in 1887 in *On the Genealogy of Morals,*

> all superior men who were irresistibly drawn to throw
> off the yoke of any kind of morality and to frame new
> laws had, if they were not actually mad, no alternative
> but to make themselves or pretend to be mad—and
> this indeed applies to innovators in every domain and
> not only in the domain of priestly and political
> dogma . . . —"how can one make oneself mad when
> one is not mad and does not dare to appear so?"—

almost all the significant men of ancient civilization
have pursued this train of thought.

It would be simple-minded to see this as a critique of
sanity, or indeed as a historically accurate account of
what Nietzsche calls, so approvingly, "ancient civilization." He is instead using this fictional history to describe
a kind of passion for stasis, a lethargic, reactionary resistance to change—a protection of certain vested interests
against the possibility of a more vital life—that he saw in
the presumably "inferior" men who were his contemporaries. Madness, he suggests, is an ambition for anyone
who wants any kind of moral innovation or improvisa-
tion. "All earlier people," he writes, "found it much more
likely that wherever there is madness there is also a grain
of genius and wisdom"—the implication being that
wherever there is sanity, or too little madness, there is always the dull, the uninspired, and the traditional. Sanity
is the pose of those who want to keep things the same; it
has become, by the end of the nineteenth century, the an-
tithesis of wisdom because it is the enemy of the new. It is
part of the new wisdom to believe that sanity is slavish;
that the sane are the disciples of a new bourgeois fundamentalism, the fundamentalism of security. The new
problem is how to become sufficiently mad—how to

break down this reactionary sanity—in order to make new laws. Less dramatically, Nietzsche is also drawing our attention to the fact that we are likely to call mad all those people who do things that unsettle us, that destroy something of the past in us. Sane becomes our word now for all those people who don't trouble us, but reassure us. The most interesting thing about other people, the most valuable thing about other people, Nietzsche intimates, is the kind of problems they pose us. Do they reinsure our past, secure our assumptions; or do they threaten our cherished past, revise it to make a new kind of future? And these are precisely the problems posed by a person we desire. A sane choice, a choice that makes too much sense, spells fear of the uncertainty of the future.

Nietzsche's rather literary idealization of madness and his implied caricature of sanity show, if nothing else, that in his view modern people were terrorized by change. Change can be talked up by describing it as progress or development; or it can be talked down by calling it disintegration and loss. Those implicated as sane, for Nietzsche, are those who are acknowledging, by trying to freeze-frame their lives, the full horror of enduring change unsponsored by a God and his Providence. When madness is ennobled, "sanity" becomes a dirty word.

At puberty the reemergence of sexual desire changes the adolescent too much—more than she can possibly cope with. The old passion for the parents becomes a new passion for the new. And despite one's wishes, despite the relentlessness of one's quest for parental figures, there are no new parents. Like Nietzsche's "superior men," the adolescent acquires and requires a madness to broach the disturbing innovation called adulthood. Puberty, which no one ever recovers from any more than they recover from the sexuality that ushers it in, is everyone's first experience of a sentient madness. Sanity is a story told by the survivors. Sanity, if it comes at all, comes afterward.

III. Available Madness

JUST AS the whole notion of sanity was coming more and more into circulation—at least for the medical profession—another very strange idea was gaining currency toward the end of the nineteenth century in Europe. It was an idea familiar from Greek tragedy to the few who had been privileged with a classical education; and one that was to be confirmed by the unprecedented horrors of the twentieth century. This was the idea that if Man—as people were still called—was to know himself as he really was, he would go mad; or he would discover himself to be in fact mad. Whether this idea—which so much of Western culture is based on—was described as Man's newfound animal nature, as promoted by Darwin and Freud; or in terms of the relentless brutality of Marx's class war; or just in terms of an ineluctable and unpredictable genetic determinism at work in a carefree law-bound cosmos; what there was to know was not reassuring for the self-knowing, self-cherishing self. The promise of Romanticism, of the progressive, developing, mysteriously fascinating self that was supposed to be everyone's birthright—and that was there to be loved and cultivated and, of course, known—began to look like nothing special in the light of new scientific discoveries. It was more like an old-style curse than a newfangled gift. This disillusionment, which has been so difficult to turn to account, to transform into something either inspiring or consoling, made the traditionally hallowed quest for self-knowledge a dangerously mixed blessing. And it made all the previously available versions of sanity sound, at their worst, like more or less benign forms of self-deception. It was the art of not knowing who one was, the subtle ruses and accomplishments of ignorance—all the modern forms of anesthesia would be in this category: money, sex, drugs, success, work, etc.—that began to be viewed by Marxists and Freudians, among many others, as the only available contemporary saving graces. Sanity meant finding ways of not knowing about all the things that might drive you insane were you to know them. The modern individual has to be always as efficient as possible at arranging his ignorance.

The exponential growth of scientific knowledge about the world, and of scientific ways of knowing, in the past two centuries had to be shadowed by the most artful avoidances of knowledge about what had traditionally been called the "human heart." The poet Robert Lowell, in "Waking Early Sunday Morning" (1967), tracks this distinctively modern apprehension of what we hear about ourselves when the consolations of our familiar religions grow faint:

> . . . But what if a new
> diminuendo brings no true
> tenderness, only restlessness,
> excess, the hunger for success,
> sanity of self-deception
> fixed and kicked by restless caution,
> while we listen to the bells . . .

Lowell suggests that a better sanity would involve a "true tenderness." Sanity, it should be noted, is more often linked with kindness than with truth. But the only sanity now available is a self-deceiving one. And the deceit of the modern self—a self fashioned for evasions rather than apprehensions—issues in restlessness, excess, and an insatiable appetite for success. Sanity of a kind is recruited, is all too easily recruitable, as part of modern armory. What is being pursued when sanity is pursued, what is done in the name of sanity, can be a self-blinding.

If sanity runs the risk of becoming another word for self-deception, what then does this make madness? What kind of life would the self-undeceived live? Once sanity becomes a repertoire of avoidances—and it is surprisingly difficult for it not to become that: most people don't encourage their children to join cults, for example—we are left wondering not only what sanity might feel like, but what sanity must be like if it is so vulnerable to the things it is vulnerable to. Lowell's modern "sanity of self-deception" suggests that we are in a bind, and our versions of sanity may be part of the problem, rather than part of the solution. (Lowell's lines have not only the weight of eloquence, but also the weight of experience: Lowell gave no glamour to his own bouts of clinical insanity.) We may claim that we want to know ourselves, that we value above all an intelligent familiarity with ourselves; and we may claim that we want to be sane and are most horrified by the mad, but knowing ourselves and being sane may be mutually exclusive. In which case, the only sanity available to us now may be the madness, the utter mystification, of self-deception. ("One lies more to oneself than to others," Byron once wrote in a letter.) These, at least, have become our modern suspicions.

There are three modern conditions, three modern psychiatric diagnoses—childhood autism, schizophrenia, and depression—that have challenged our always measured wish to know the extremes of human unhappiness and that speak vividly of our contemporary fears of insanity. As we shall see, despite the patent differences between these conditions—and the contemporary debates in competing disciplines about their diagnosis and treatment—it is striking how much consensus there is about just what it is, apparently, to be a healthy, sane, modern person. Of course, there can only be a debate at all about causes and cures, about natures and nurtures because the interested parties agree, more or less, in their descriptions of these conditions. One of the things that modern disciplines agree to do is to describe the insane in terms of what they are unable to do. When the mad are not being all too starkly idealized, they tend to be assessed according to their deficits. To be diagnosed as autistic or depressed, schizoid or perverse is to be seen to be lacking in what are considered to be the essential qualities of a normal sane person: communicativeness, vitality, warmth, and humaneness. But surprisingly often we have to infer what the sane must be like from what it is to be mad. Discussions of sanity and madness are always discussions about what people want people to be and to like. Like any moral discourse these discussions involve competing claims about what people should be capable of being.

ONE OF THE most poignant and disarming things about spending any time with an autistic child is that it is like being in a room with someone who only appears to be a person; or who has forgotten how to be one. It is not merely that the child seems to be utterly self-absorbed— far removed from even the glimmerings of contact with anyone else; it is as though the child has no self to be absorbed in or by. It is like being with someone who is concentrating very hard, but who has nothing to concentrate on. Unlike an ordinary child when he sulks, a child in this state doesn't seem disappointed. He isn't, as the adults might say, disillusioned because it is as though he never had any illusions to begin with. In order to sustain any therapeutic hope with such children, one finds oneself imagining analogies: it is like being with someone who has been buried alive; it is like being with someone who is in solitary confinement, but that no one, including themselves, knows about this; it is like being with someone who is not bereft, not homesick or grief-stricken, because he has never been attached to something or someone he could lose. It is you—the other person—who feels lost or left or confounded. The autistic child, one imagines at one's most despondent, has got nothing to lose from contact with another person, and therefore has nothing to gain either. Given that children evoke our most intense feelings—children are the people we almost always want to give something to—what is so devastating about being in the absent presence of an autistic child is the feeling of irrelevance; not merely of being nothing special to the child, but of being nothing. It is not that the child doesn't seem to want anything, it's that wanting seems never to have occurred to him.

In childhood autism, Frances Tustin, a child psychotherapist, writes,

> auto-sensuousness holds sway, attention being focused almost exclusively on bodily rhythms and sensations. Objects in the outside world may be attended to (often, as it seems, intently and in minute detail), but on close observation it becomes clear that these are being experienced as part of the body or very closely akin to it. People or things outside are scarcely used or seen as having a separate existence. . . . In short, autism is a state in which experience is not differentiated or objectivised to any appreciable extent.
>
> (*Autistic States in Children*, 1981)

For the autistic child the world is his body, and his body is neither a source of pleasure nor of nourishment. It is not that the child is unable or unwilling to recognize objects and people as separate, as different from himself; it is that, from his point of view, there are no objects and people there to be separate. Because there is no elsewhere for the child—in fantasy or in reality—there is nowhere for him to be (we are always where we are in relation to some imagined, some defining other place). Just as a child cannot give himself a cuddle, pick himself up, or hold himself, the autistic child cannot even try to mother himself—to replace the mother out of rage and disappointment; he is living as if there was and is no such thing as a mother, as though such a creature had never existed. In a state of unbearable anguish the autistic child has to survive at the cost of his own growth. The child literally seems to be holding himself together through his minute, obsessive forms of attention (as if concentrating to stop oneself from disintegrating). These children are oblivious in a way that "obliviates" the people around them, making them feel that their capacity to love has never existed, and could never work even if it did. "I call autistic children 'shell-type' or 'encapsulated children,'" Tustin writes:

> Their parents often say such things as, "I can't reach him." "My child seems to be in a shell all the time." "It's as though he can't see or hear us, or won't." Such children are often thought to be deaf and some even try to walk through objects as if they were blind. However, on being tested, their perceptual apparatus is found to be intact; it is the processing of incoming information that is faulty. This could be due to brain lesions or to psychogenic damage. . . . This psychogenic

damage causes autistic children to turn their attention
away from the things that the developing child usually
attends to. This seems to be because they are protecting their bodies from "not-me" threats which are felt
to be overwhelmingly dangerous. When working with
these children it becomes clear that anything which is
not familiar, and is "not-me" arouses intense terror.

(*Autistic Barriers in Neurotic Patients,* 1987)

Autistic children are people whose attention one cannot attract, and who, to all intents and purposes, do not
themselves seem to be seeking attention. It is the paradoxical effect of such a condition that it attracts, if not by
intention, considerable attention that isn't recognized as
such by those suffering from the condition and so cannot
be used by them. (Attention seeking is one of the surest
signs of life that is called hope.) And these children require excessive attentive protection because their sense
apparatus is unavailable; they are endangered by their
lack of awareness. Their terror of everything that is not
themselves makes the so-called world a place in which
one needs a shell, and that shell, that encapsulation, is often found in rituals of obsessive, minute attention, or the
frantic clinging to specific but meaningless objects. (This
is not unlike, of course, some people's relationship to

their work, which is sometimes the work of staving off one's need for the world of other people.) The autistic child lives as if there is no world, no meaning, no pleasure, and nothing to do except those things they have to do to stave off the terror of being alive.

In Tustin's view, childhood autism, as developed in infancy, is "a massive formation of avoidance reactions in order to deal with a traumatic awareness of bodily separateness from their mother. This impinged upon [the infant's] awareness before their psychic apparatus was ready to take the strain." A "traumatic awareness of bodily separateness" from the mother has to be pictured as the rupturing of connection to a life-support system. All the behaviors and supposed states of mind referred to by the word "autism" are the child's attempts at self-cure, at damage limitation. The child, in a sense, has to find a way of surviving himself; of living without the person who was there before the rupture. Everyone reenacts something of this in any separation; and Tustin rightly refers to what she calls, quaintly, "autistic pockets" in so-called normal people. It may, in other words, be part of being a modern person to experience some degree of trauma in one's separation from the mother's body; as though no one could ever be quite ready for this. And autistic or autisticlike solutions have to be found for being so far out on a limb; for being forced to live before you have a life to do it in.

As well as the trauma of precocious separation there is the trauma of the child's solution. What is traumatic about the child's solution—about the autistic symptoms of encapsulation, remoteness, frantic self-containment—is that it is a self-thwarting kind of self-reliance; a self-reliance in which there is no self to rely on. It is a situation in which nothing comes of nothing; there is repetitiveness, but no innovation or development, because the future is also the unfamiliar, the not-me. The autistic child is holding on to what he's barely got; nothing can be done when there's nowhere to go.

One implication of this is that a child's sanity—the well-being that makes development possible—involves a capacity for wholehearted dependence. It is clearly sane for the child to be able to use the resources that are necessary, and available, for his growth. This sanity depends though upon particular forms of exchange taking place between mother and child. The sane child, in other words, needs to develop in a way that ensures that he can recognize and have access to the things that he needs, and that are therefore good for him. The sane child should know a good thing when he sees one. But if he is prematurely separated from the mother, it is as though he is stripped of a skin—he is left so unprotected from his needs, so unheld, that he must effectively blank them out. The insane child has no viable experience of dependence, and is then prone to depend upon things—ritualistic acts, forms of attention, insignificant objects as extensions of his own body—that give him an existence but not a life. To be sane is to be nourishable; and sanity depends essentially upon the kinds of exchange—the kinds of proximity and use of the mother's body—that facilitate development. The good, of which everything else is a part—the mother, the child, their appetite for each other, and for other things and people—can be called growth. Or, rather, development of a particular sort: development in the direction of revealing the benefits of the interdependence of human beings on each other. It is sane to believe in, and to live as if there are, good things and people in the world that can help us live our lives. It is sane to be capable of and to get pleasure from innovation, spontaneity, responsiveness, and change. It is sane to be intelligible enough and appealing enough to another to get one's needs met. It is sane not to render other people redundant and invisible. What the sane human being cannot be is desperate, terrorized, or remote. Above all, a sane child or a child developing toward sanity must be able to live out and live through his appetites; but to do this he has to be a producer of the shareable signs and meanings that our culture has equipped his parents to recognize, and be looked after by sufficiently receptive and responsive adults. In Tustin's accurate account of what autistic children are like, autism is about distance. The child needs to have a certain kind of access to the mother. And, by implication, insofar as adulthood is deemed to be the afterlife of childhood, what keeps adults sane is proximity to something akin to the mother's body. (Once this would have been proximity to God, or to the Virtues, or to some other good; now it is likely to be a satisfying relationship.) The insane are always described as being far away from us, too out of touch with things.

In order to survive, the autistic child has to appear to stop wanting. He survives by not living what we think of as a life. Everything parents might want from a child is denied them. Everything a child might want from his parents is foreclosed. It is always callous to use anyone as an example of anything; and anyone who has known an autistic child knows the desolation and frustration and panic these children live in. But we need to consider as we look at these contemporary predicaments our assumptions about normalization. If sanity is taken to be a useful norm—a guideline when no one can be sure what our best lines are—we should be asking of any so-called pathology, of any symptom: what is it a cure for, what is the predicament that makes it necessary? What could someone be hoping for when he exhibits this symptom, and why has his desire had to take this form? There is, it would seem, no imaginable world in which it would be sane to be autistic; but for the autistic child there is no imaginable world in which it would be sane (i.e., safe) to be anything else.

The norm that is silently spelled out to us in accounts of childhood autism is clearly one in which wanting works; a world of communion and not isolation; a world of reciprocal pleasures and easy communication. The normal child can be soothed and satisfied, enjoyed and fought with. The sane mother and child, one could say, are not too terrified of each other. They can get on with each other to get their growing done. In this picture, which itself isolates mother and child from their surrounding world, what neither of them can know much about is the partly untraceable consensus, the cultural agreement about normality that they have inherited. It is terrible to be an autistic child; but it can also be terrible to assume that human wanting is the kind of thing that can be efficiently communicated, and thoroughly known about. If sanity is defined by how intelligible we are to each other, then we are living under tremendous pressure to be as transparent as possible. The problem may not be always or only how to better understand each other (and ourselves), but actually what we should do with whatever we don't understand.

"TO THE SCHIZOPHRENIC INDIVIDUAL," the psycho-analyst Harold Searles writes in his work *Counter-transference* (1979), "the question has been not how but whether to relate to his fellow man and, through becoming familiar with his views, we realize that in us too this has been, all along, a meaningful and alive and continuing conflict, heretofore hidden from ourselves."

Whatever the causes of schizophrenia—and explanations have ranged since the late nineteenth century from degeneration through to genetics, from syphilis to inconsistent parenting—descriptions of the effect of the so-called schizophrenic on those looking after him are remarkably similar. They stress that the person who is deemed to be schizophrenic has found bizarre ways of not relating to people. He is someone so engrossed by the futility of collaboration, someone so determinedly or definitively inaccessible that in the history of psychiatry and the psychotherapies the schizophrenic has been a kind of cause célèbre, and schizophrenia has become the exemplary modern instance of insanity.

What everyone agrees about the schizophrenic, even when they disagree about virtually everything else, is that even when he tries to speak he has trouble making himself understood. "Despair," Leslie Farber wrote, "is more or less intrinsic to the therapeutic life as it involves schizophrenia" (*The Ways of the Will*, 1966). And this despair is over the possibility of having any significant or useful contact; a despair, that is, over the possibility of there being any shared worlds.

Yet it is schizophrenia, as a contemporary predicament, that has inspired some of the most eloquent and impassioned writing from the psychiatric and antipsychiatric professions. Working with schizophrenic patients can make people fervent about what the mad can say—often by not speaking, or by not speaking in the usual ways—that the supposedly sane don't want to hear. This implies that sanity in its modern versions, in its most successful performances of itself, is a steering clear of specific doubts about the self (self-doubt may be good, but our sanity can't take too much of it). To be sane now, in other words, might be to take too many things for granted.

"The man in the street," R. D. Laing wrote in *Self and Others* (1961),

> takes a lot for granted: for instance, that he has a body
> which has an inside and an outside; that he has begun at
> his birth and ends, biologically speaking, at his death;

that he occupies a position in space; that he occupies a position in time; that he exists as a continuous being from one place to the next and from one moment to another. The ordinary person does not reflect upon these basic elements of his being; he takes his way of experiencing himself and others to be "true." However, some people do not. They are often called schizoid. Still more, the schizophrenic does not take for granted his own person (and other persons) as being an adequately embodied, alive, real, substantial and continuous being, who is at one place at one time and a different place at a different time, remaining the "same" throughout. In the absence of this "base" he lacks the usual sense of personal unity, a sense of himself as the agent of his own actions rather than as a robot, a machine, a thing, and of being the author of his own perceptions, but rather feels that someone else is using his eyes, his ears.

The critique of "normal" sanity always wants to persuade us that it is based on a precarious sense of entitlement; that taking things for granted is always taking too much for granted. What the schizoid person lacks—a sense of a boundaried, substantial body, continuity in space and time, a feeling of spontaneous agency, an unquestioning—provides us with a guide to sanity. Everyone may have some of these experiences some of the time; but for these to be the defining experiences in a life is grounds for concern. And yet putting it plainly, as Laing does—offering us, in a sense, the double life of the man in the street; the assured life and the confounded life—it is the hard work of sanity, the unrelenting need not to be mad, that is so striking. The man in the street, like the sane man, has been rigged up to stop us asking whether it is worth relating to other people; whether it is normal to want to be normal. It is possible, Searles, Farber, and Laing all intimate, to have suffered in childhood in ways that make so-called sanity too severe a demand on the individual. It is possible for a person to have experiences that lead him to believe that such sanity as he has resides in his ability to stop himself from having any more experiences. Like childhood autism, adult schizophrenia speaks of a despair about the beneficence of human exchange. It seems to prevent the process of both giving and being given to. While it is insane to be unintelligible, it is sometimes sane, in the sense of self-protective or safe, to insulate oneself, to remove oneself from the dominion of others. It is also insane, in the sense of too distressing to those others, to be ungraspable, beyond negotiation, manipulation, or coercion. People are called insane when their behavior renders others impotent. It is sane, in other words, not to make other people feel resourceless.

Faced with these extremities of suffering and incomprehension, sanity becomes part of an extensive vocabulary of reassurance. It reassures us that people have the resources—the talents, the gifts, the patience, the resilience—to deal with whatever people can become and with whatever people can do to each other. In the descriptions of Tustin and Laing it is not the so-called morality of these individuals that is at stake—whether they are nice people or cruel people, what their ethical ambitions for themselves and others are—but their strangeness. It is as though they are before good and evil, struggling to survive, not to be good, to stay intact in order not to impress anyone. Because they lack the basic assumptions of sanity—the belief that they are like other people, and that there are other people; the belief that there is such a thing as a good exchange; the belief that pleasure exists and that it is pleasurable—they are beyond reach.

It is part of the ethos of each of these writers to assume not simply that there are people who are schizophrenic or autistic and people who are not, but also to assume that these conditions are all part of the modern human repertoire of feelings. A false sanity, or a precarious version of sanity, will tell us that the sane are people who are not mad; whereas a better vision of sanity would include experiencing and acknowledging these madder parts of the self. In this way, those madder parts of the self—the autistic solutions to separation, the sense of being controlled, of having no boundaries—are more like modern human predispositions, talents for dealing with the unbearable. Thus, not being able to be mad, not being able to have recourse to mad solutions, would itself be a disability. Sanity in its narrower definitions deprives us of some necessary tools. It allows us neither our full range of emotional reactions to situations—whether terror, bewilderment, or ecstasy—nor our most effective forms of self-protection against them.

Sanity, as the project of keeping ourselves recognizably human, therefore has to limit the range of human experience. To keep faith with recognition we have to stay recognizable. Sanity, in other words, becomes a pressing preoccupation as soon as we recognize the importance of recognition. When we define ourselves by what we can recognize, by what we can comprehend—rather than, say, by what we can describe—we are continually under threat from what we are unwilling and/or unable to see. We are tyrannized by our blind spots, and by whatever it is about ourselves that we find unacceptable.

THE DEATH-IN-LIFE that is depression, the poverty and the depletion and the feelinglessness that can take people over, is a horrifying reminder of how obscure the sources of our energy are. Both the chemical and the more psychological accounts of the causes of and treatments for depression are unavoidably exercised by the question of what vitalizes a life, what it is that makes life seem worth living; and, by the same token, what has to happen in a person's life that makes him prone to a sense of futility—to feeling defeated by the tragedies, frustrations, and obstacles that his life presents him with. The healthier person, with whom the depressed person is being compared—and who the depressed person, when he is not too depressed, aspires to be—is inspired by difficulties to transform him and is zealous about pleasure rather than dismayed by it; he has the energy to feel things and is given energy by what he feels. The sane person has found, or been given, a way of loving life that has made the whole question of whether life is lovable seemingly irrelevant. Once again the sane person takes for granted everything that the depressed person feels is lacking in his life. He has either found a way of living that makes the problems disappear or is just the kind of person to whom such problems never occur. The depressed person is always capable, if he has sufficient life in him, to envy the undepressed. Unlike the autistic child and the schizophrenic adult, there is no doubt in the depressed person's mind that other people exist; it is just that their existence cannot lighten or enlighten him. He seems to be driven by a lack of desire, by a lacklusterness that cannot be willed away. He may not want to die, but he cannot always find a good reason for wanting to be alive—or indeed muster an interest in reasons at all.

It is rarely assumed that not wanting to live might be part of wanting to live; or that finding one's life—or as it is usually generalized in such states of mind, finding life itself—unbearable may, in certain circumstances, be the sane option, the utterly realistic view. The chemical explanations for depression assume that it is normal and necessary to have the requisite chemicals to keep one's spirits up; and so depression is, as they say, a chemical imbalance. More mechanistic psychological explanations describe it as a dysfunction: in the more normal functioning of the organism the dominant mood would not be depression, and so one might learn less depressed and less depressing ways of functioning. More psychoanalytic descriptions seek to persuade us that depression is an inevitable and therefore normal reaction to certain developmental experiences, if not actually a developmental achievement itself. Thus a capacity to be depressed means being able to recognize something that is true— that development involves loss and separation, that we hurt people we love and need—and that we are prepared to bear the grief and guilt. In this sense, depression makes us real. It deepens us.

Even modern anatomies of melancholy agree with Thomas Burton's *Anatomy of Melancholy* of 1621, that vitality is unpredictable and that it has a cause, whether God, a life force, chemistry, or instincts. They agree that depression has a meaning or a purpose, but they also ask: is depression—which is staggeringly prevalent in contemporary Western societies—integral to a life, one of the occupational hazards of living a life now in particular societies, one of the ways people cope (Winnicott once referred to depression as the "fog over the battlefield")? Or is it something akin to a malfunction, and of no possible use or benefit to the person who suffers from it (we don't think of a flat tire as any kind of advantage to a car)? "The opposite of depression," Andrew Solomon, a sufferer, writes in his recent memoir, *The Noonday Demon,* "is not happiness but vitality"—and without vitality there is literally no life. It is not that life is better when one has some vitality, it is that without vitality there is no life.

Given that depression as a contemporary malady is universally feared, it is of great interest that there is, in the modern period, at least one group of people—called, broadly speaking, Kleinian psychoanalysts—for whom the capacity to be depressed, though not depression as a way of life, has been the defining feature of their version of sanity. Calling it the Depressive Position, and describing it as a sign of what they think of as emotional maturity, they make a case for a preferred state of mind, that everyone, in their view, struggles to achieve and to sustain. In the shift that is said to occur in the Depressive Position there is a move toward what the psychoanalyst Hannah Segal calls "sane functioning . . . the sense of psychic reality develops—acknowledging and assuming responsibility for one's impulses." The "values" of the Depressive Position, another psychoanalyst, Donald Meltzer, writes, involve "the relinquishment of egocentricity in favor of concern for the welfare of the loved objects." Depression here becomes another word for the individual seeing what he is really like both inside and outside, what he does to the people he loves by virtue of the desires he has, and becoming more concerned about his impact upon them. This is depression not as lack of vitality so much as disillusionment with the self. What it shares with depression in the more ordinary use of the term is that it involves a catastrophic loss of self-love. And it implies a newfound keenness to look after and protect the people and things that one loves. What is lost in both versions of depression, however, is the idea of self as idol, of the self as worthy of admiration to itself.

Seen through the prism of depression, sanity is always bound up with self-regard. From childhood autism and schizophrenia we can get a picture of the sane self as intelligible about its wants, as seeming to live within some consensus of shared desires and meanings and forms of exchange. From depression we get a sense of the sane self as loving itself in the right way, of having what is considered to be appropriate self-regard: the kind of feeling about oneself that sustains one's appetite for life. This vitality, moreover, is likely to issue in finding objects of love, and then having the wherewithal to protect one's cake and eat it. In this picture, too much or too little self-love will render one insane. Sanity means loving oneself in exactly the right way, or knowing exactly what it is about oneself that is worth loving. This means, essentially, having a self—believing in a picture, or a story, or a set of preferred fantasies—to love. Whether you need a self to go mad, or whether madness is construed as a loss of self, or even puts the whole notion of a definitive self in question, has always been an issue when madness is discussed. Sanity usually implies the existence of a self. It takes a self for granted. Indeed, this is often the sane self to which madness plays the antiself.

Depression, as a pathology, illuminates vitality, passion, and engagement as the qualities of a saner, preferred self. The sane are neither apathetic nor lethargic. They are not lacking in enthusiasm. They are not killjoys.

But the risk of this view is that the sane self is assumed to be stronger than any circumstances that might confront it. For example, there are situations in which it might be sane—as in, realistic—to be depressed (in a famine, or in isolation, or deprived of sympathetic interest). One of the greatest confusions surrounding the notion of the sane self as we infer it from the available pathologies is whether or not sanity is about being in touch with reality. Faced with certain realities it would be, in a real sense, sane to be autistic, schizoid, or depressed. Is sanity by definition the refusal to be driven mad, the unwillingness to adopt mad solutions? Or is it the self-serving talent for adopting the solutions of madness? Is it the freedom to dispense with the repertoire of madness or the freedom to use this repertoire as a psychological toolkit when necessary?

Perhaps we should value sanity now for the questions it forces us to face about how we want to live and who we want to be. It can make us wonder not merely how we can temper the unacceptable things about ourselves, but also how we can release the good things, the things that matter most to us. So we must turn now to what happens to our ideas about sanity when money matters most to us.

IV. Money Mad

WHEN THE ACCUMULATION of wealth is no longer of high social importance," the economist J. M. Keynes wrote in 1932,

there will be great changes in the code of morals. We shall be able to rid ourselves of many of the pseudo-moral principles that have hagridden us for two hundred years, by which we have exalted some of the most distasteful human qualities into the position of the highest virtues. We shall be able to afford to dare to assess the money-motive at its true value. The love of money as a possession—as distinguished from the love of money as a means to the enjoyments and realities of life—will be recognized for what it is . . . one of those . . . semi-pathological propensities which one hands over with a shudder to the specialists in mental disease.

(*Essays in Persuasion*)

The "money-motive," which Keynes suggests we are too frightened to assess, is a kind of moral alchemy, a magical act in which the bad is made to seem good; in which what was once considered to be most distasteful about people—the callous ruthlessness of their greed, say— begins to be described as morally impressive (realistic, bold, ingenious, and so on). When this relatively new transvaluation of all values comes to an end, when we finally see through the accumulation of wealth as a paramount project, we will have something akin to a secular revelation, Keynes hopes. The love of money will be revealed as an aberration, a form of madness by which we were temporarily assailed. In this extraordinary utopian fantasy, the most successful people in the culture, the rich, will be handed over to the only people who know how to treat them, the specialists in mental disease. There had been a moral catastrophe, Keynes believed; the mad are ruling the world. The sane will be those who dare to assess the money-motive.

What the desire for money has been a desire for has never been clear. What one is loving when one loves money begs all the questions. Power, prestige, security, invulnerability, independence, glamour—all these ideals involve us in an infinite regress of asking in turn what each of these may represent a desire for. We must ask how and why we have come to think of them as worth wanting; and what we must be like as creatures if such things give us pleasure, if for such things we are prepared to sacrifice so much else. The money-motive—and money as an object of desire, and the material wealth and influence it brings with it—has always been shadowed by a counter culture of suspicion and fear; trailed by skeptical commentaries in which the desire for money reveals the very worst aspects of modern human appetite. Money, like sexuality, reveals to us something peculiarly disturbing, even pathological, about the nature of our desires.

The money-motive for Keynes is an internal saboteur of all that could and should be best about human nature. With the invention of money, he implies, a new kind of pleasure entered the world; a pleasure that resembles sexuality in that it can drive people crazy; people will risk their lives and their supposedly better selves for it. But if it reveals the insanity, what Keynes calls the "semi-criminal, semi-pathological propensities" of so-called human nature, it also, by the same token, implies a saner human nature, one undistracted by the love of money, refusing to consent to the money-motive. If money is appetite by another name, our love for it may tell us more about our appetite than our appetite can tell us about our love of money. Rather than being a love akin to other loves, a love for money may be a new kind of love altogether—a love that destroys the capacity for all the other kinds of love that preceded it.

It is a striking fact that sanity—or what Keynes refers to as "the highest virtues"—has rarely been associated with wealth. In our always too-bland imaginings of the sane they are by definition never driven by the money-motive. They are the people who could never love money, for whom the phrase itself would be a contradiction in terms. It is not exactly that the rich are expected to be mad—though they are, of course, freer to be what is politely called eccentric, freer to indulge their tastes and temperaments, however cruel—nor that poverty is assumed, at least these days, to be anything other than utterly degrading and debilitating. But it is generally assumed that, as motives go, the financial doesn't tend to bring out the best in people. There has traditionally been a connection between wealth and corruption (i.e., cruelty), between the desire for money and versions of human behavior that we can sometimes only afford to be secretly impressed by. The money-motive, for example, has helped us to keep believing in Original Sin, or its secular equivalents. When wealth is not being blatantly celebrated as it is in the money cult we now live in, it is usually described as an object of desire that has waylaid us from a better course in life. The desire for money in this account becomes the desire that sabotages, that betrays all the other, better, desires; that makes them look both old-fashioned and unrealistic. In the alchemy described by Keynes, fairness becomes naiveté, the kind are the exploitable, the sympathetic are the sentimentally weak, and so on. It is not merely that the money-motive reveals something we already think we know—that human appetite, at its most extreme, is utterly self-important and cruelly self-regarding—but also that the madness of human appetite threatens so much of what we claim to value that it creates unbearable conflicts within us. We don't want to kill the things we love, we want to make them suffer. If you kill someone, after all, you can't go on exploiting him.

Keynes's nostalgic utopianism reminds us that all of the so-called great world religions contain stories about the ways in which the accumulation of wealth can distract people from the best lives that are actually available to them. The appetite for possession is a peculiarly tyrannical species of bodily appetite, at once hypnotic and exacting, and there have always been parallel texts to those recording the growth of empires and the uncanny expansions and expansiveness of capitalism (of which Marxism and various versions of Primitive Christianity have been the most forceful in the West). These counternarratives tell us that profiteering, exploitation, and ownership are not expressions of human appetite but perversions of it.

We should not be tempted into believing that there is something natural and normal about the insatiability of our appetites. It is possible, they tell us, not to want more than we need; and not to assume that we know what we want. But each and all of these critiques and counter-claims share an acknowledgment; which is that in human beings, apparently unlike all other animals, appetite can destroy the best things about appetite. It can in fact destroy appetite itself. Human beings can even get pleasure from ruining their own and other people's appetites. The love of money is especially good at exposing the insanity of human desires. Its exorbitance, its carelessness, its brutality, its shortsightedness; the guilt that makes it so aggressive, and the aggression that can make it so unnegotiable; all are revealed.

To desire money more than anything else, or to let money stand in for all that we desire, tells us more about desiring than it does about money. (We often have to invent an object of desire in order to understand something new about our desiring.) The fact that the passionate "natural" appetite of the human infant—for food, affection, recognition, protection, curiosity, rage, and so on—can so quickly and easily become a love for money, and for what money can buy, suggests that the primary desire for modern Westerners may simply be to be able to go on desiring; to go on believing in, and being sustained by, appetite. Since money always promises something other than itself—it is only, as we say, worth what it can buy—it seems to protect us, as promises do, from the fear of there being nothing and no one that we want. Nothing around that makes appetite—or its derivatives, faith, hope, curiosity—worth having. Money gives people an appetite for appetite. Not desiring is far more daunting a prospect than the unavailability of what one desires. A world in which there is scarcity of need, a world in which wanting is a futile passion, is more terrifying than a world in which there is scarcity of resources.

Keynes warns us that accumulation of wealth is driving us mad, but reminds us, by the same token, that it would be sane to want an alternative. If we are not to be, in his grim terms, "disgustingly morbid," "semi-criminal," and "semi-pathological"; if we are not to be "hag-ridden" by "pseudo-moral principles" engendered by the love of money as a possession, then we are going to have to find something else to love. The sanity he prescribes means love of the right good things.

It would also be part of our sanity, Keynes suggests, to dare to assess the money-motive at its true value; as though the assessment of this motive were itself the breaking of a taboo, or could put us at some kind of risk. The desire for money, Keynes makes quite clear, is a desire for something essentially perverse, and our sanity resides in facing the facts about it. Only by seeing it for what it is can we recover our moral health. Sanity always brings with it a notion of moral well-being that apparently comes from seeing things as they are. Because they are undeceived the sane are undeceiving. What, one wonders, were people like, in Keynes's view, two hundred years ago, before the money madness apparently took over? (The sane, as so often, are rarely contemporary; they are figments, what the anthropologist Edward Tylor, writing in the nineteenth century, called "survivals" from the past.) And what would people be like when they finally get over the madness of the money-motive?

ONE OF THE WAYS in which people have traditionally tried to understand money, and to retain their sanity about it, has been to think in terms of what money can't buy. Money, perhaps, can be useful as a negative ideal in freeing us, by its very existence, to wonder both what we would be wanting if we didn't want money and what it may be that we need, which no amount of money could ever get for us. When the young Paul Dombey, in a famous scene in Dickens's *Dombey and Son* (1848), asks his father, "What's money . . . what can it do?" and is told, by way of reply, that it "can do anything," the child says, on cue, "I wonder why it didn't save me my mama."

Money, we are reminded, has never stopped people from dying; and children, we are reminded, would rather have their parents than an accumulation of wealth. That money can't buy everything that matters doesn't of course mean that it can't buy anything that matters. But what Dickens, like many of his contemporaries, is trying to work out is what it is about money that makes it such an utterly compelling, wholly persuasive object of desire. How, Dickens wonders, will the child with an ineluctable passion for his parents become the adult who will do virtually anything for money? The changeover from love of the parents to love of money became an emblem in nineteenth-century novels not merely for growing up as the loss of innocence, but for growing up as the loss of sanity.

As Keynes knew, people have always been "able to afford to dare to assess the money-motive at its true value." Money is, virtually by definition, the value whose value is always in question because money is only what it is deemed to be worth. Its value is thus peculiarly difficult to assess. But from the New Testament ("... there are so many things which cash will not pay! Cash is a great miracle; yet it has not all power in heaven, nor even on earth"); and from the Desert Fathers to Karl Marx, the true value of the money-motive, we are told, is that it destroys value. And because the appetite for money involves destroying so much that we value, it is taken to be, in secular terms, an appetite allied to madness. (Insanity is traditionally linked to excess, but an excess of money is a sign of success.) The love of money becomes the love that makes us betray our other loves, and yet because the money-motive is socially sanctioned and rewarded, love of money becomes an unofficial form of madness, at once admired and distrusted. Making money means mixing one's labor with the world's, and involvement with this world corrupts one's commitment to the next world. Profit requires exploitation, and exploitation is morally unacceptable. The Good Life, however conceived, always entails having the right amount of money, and loving the right things. If love of money makes us mad and bad, then in which direction does our sanity lie? One of the ways in which we can tell whether someone is sane is by their relationship, as it is so often called, to money. Money, like sexuality, is one of the things that every sane person would have to have thought about. What, after all, do we think our sanity is—how do we picture it at work—if love of money is one of the things that can so easily undo it? The sane, presumably, can resist the lure of money. Perhaps, indeed, they have discovered their own more pressing pleasures.

WRITING TO his friend and colleague Wilhelm Fleiss in 1898, Freud made an interesting suggestion that could only have come from his sense of the significance and formative power of childhood pleasures. "Happiness," he wrote, "is the belated fulfilment of a prehistoric wish. For this reason wealth brings so little happiness." Money is not a childhood wish. We are only really happy, Freud says, when we satisfy a childhood wish. No child has ever wanted money; therefore money doesn't really satisfy adults when they acquire it. Growing up, therefore, if it is to be satisfying, involves retaining the wishes of childhood rather than dispensing with them. Today, of course—and there could be no more telling sign of the times—there are plenty of children who want money; so we may need to rephrase this and say that no baby has ever wanted money, and the point is perhaps better made. When the gap between the pleasures of childhood and the pleasures of adulthood becomes too great, Freud implies, we become frustrated. We can even lose our will to live.

The infantile pleasures of being loved, adored, stroked, held, cuddled, infinitely attended to and responded to, and thought about; of only sleeping, eating, and playing, these are the truly satisfying pleasures. The idea that material objects, or indeed that money itself, could be any kind of alternative to these fundamental things is, Freud suggests, unrealistic. It is, in fact, a form of madness to not know, to forget, to attack and trivialize what really makes you happy. And happiness, which for Freud here is clearly akin to sanity, depends upon our being able to carry on, however cunningly, meeting our prehistoric wishes, the wishes we had before we could ever have a history of our wishes, in adulthood. The sane adult is always smuggling his childhood into the future, refashioning his childhood pleasures as legitimate adult interests. And this means not being fooled about what these wishes actually were.

For Freud the sane adult is willingly, and to some extent knowingly, the child he always was. And yet at this moment in his writing Freud was also strangely bewitched by a pastoral picture of childhood, and what seems like an implausible view of adulthood. One of the essential differences, one could say, between adults and children is that adults engage in sexual activity that children are incapable of (even if they fantasize, and wish for it). Another is that adults earn money and infants don't. There is a link, in other words, between the desire for money and so-called adult sexual desires. And what Freud has momentarily forgotten is that in his view one of the wishes of childhood, if not *the* wish of childhood, is an incestuous wish; the primary desire for the forbidden objects of desire that are the parents. One of our childhood wishes—which are the only wishes, Freud believes, that are conducive to our true happiness—is for the kind of pleasure that is essentially transgressive. People do the maddest things, the most illicit things, for love and for money; it would not be surprising if they were connected.

Adults use money to wish with. The wishes that make adults happy are childhood wishes, and the privileged wishes of childhood are transgressive. Adults usually want more money than they need, and by getting more money they can create more needs, more objects of desire, without which their lives will seem meager. And yet, Freud insists—like Keynes, but for different reasons—money doesn't quite work. Money as a now virtually universal object of adult desire—everybody wanting more, everybody never quite having enough (as children feel about their parents)—in Freud's words "brings so little happiness." In other words, what we think we want and what we actually want can be at odds with each other, and money frustrates something within us. It is strange, Freud intimates, that there are animals who do not know what they want; and that in all other creatures the continuity of their needs and wants from birth to death is self-evident. It would be a kind of madness for needs to be in doubt (imagine a world in which questions were asked about the point of breathing, or about the value of people opening their mouths). As adults in the societies in which we live we need money, but money and what it can buy leaves us feeling impoverished. For Freud it is not our morality that is at stake in the love of money, it is our happiness. It is our happiness, in his view, that keeps us sane.

We must, Freud implies, have forgotten what it is that we really want. We must be working hard not to know, not to satisfy ourselves, not to recover our pleasures (it is now the most ordinary, the most banal, form of madness to shop knowing that shopping can never satisfy many of the things we want it to). We must, in Freud's language, be repressing our wants, actively disclaiming our knowledge of what it is that we love. It is the familiar insanity of the modern person to want what she does not want; and to be able to conceal this from herself by living as if more money means more happiness.

Money, in Freud's view, presented as an object of desire, has been our most successful tool for deceiving ourselves about our own desire. To want money over and above the amount one actually needs to live is an essential part of modern people's passion for ignorance about themselves. It is what they use not only to hide their real wants from themselves—which means to secrete away their histories—but also to prevent themselves from working out what might be their heart's desire. There must be something about wanting, or something about thinking and talking about wanting, that is so dangerous that people prefer to be palmed off with substitute satisfactions; with fillers like drugs or food or money, rather than seeking out their truer pleasures. What the desire for money reveals to Freud is our hatred of happiness; our fear of satisfaction; our phobia of childhood. When it comes to what we most want, money is a bind. Our love of material possessions is a hatred of what we love. Money is the betrayal of childhood.

UNDER THE WORD "madness" the *OED* has "extravagant folly . . . ungovernable anger, rage, fury . . . extravagant excitement." There is, Freud tells us—and in this he is very much a man of his times, one of a chorus of nineteenth-century voices—an excessive violence in our desire for money; it destroys our happiness through extravagant distraction. But what Freud uses the love of money to impress upon us is that there is a madness that comes from disavowing the fact of our having been children. The love of money lures us away from the loves of childhood. It is the madness of modern human wanting not to want to know about its own wanting. Money is the emblem, for modern people, of the terror of their own desire. The sane modern adult—in that ironic reversal of values called Romanticism, of which Freud is a part—does not put away childish things. Indeed, his sanity resides in going on keeping them in circulation by refashioning them; by making them seem, to himself and others, sufficiently acceptable. This sane adult is not necessarily childish, or childlike, but he has used his adulthood to grow into his childhood and to follow its satisfactions through.

"We have to discover the origin of the money form," Marx wrote in *Das Kapital* (1867), ". . . then the enigma of money will cease to be an enigma." Freud, with a quite different project, and a quite different sense of the "origin of the money form," believed that money was the enigma we use—the enigma as fetish—to protect ourselves, to ward off the more disturbing enigmas of our desire. If the enigma of money was referred back to childhood, money was indeed—as the notorious psychoanalytic cliché has always insisted—like shit: much desired, but ultimately useless, wanted only to be dispensed with. The making of it may have its satisfactions, but the keeping and using of it do not.

THERE IS a striking paucity of explanations of the connections between so-called mental health and money. There are available norms and conventions, even though they are now by definition contentious, about our other appetites; guidelines about what it is good for us to want and why, about what is too much and what is too little; about causes and motives and consequences; about pathologies and etiquette. But when it comes to what we might call our economic appetites we are in the dark. Economists don't tend to tell us what it is about having more money that is good for us, despite the common knowledge in the affluent world that the getting of money makes more and more people crazy, and that the having of money, though "still promising to solve and satisfy" in Larkin's line, is not enough for happiness.

The great secular and religious prophets of the nineteenth century—Thomas Carlyle, John Ruskin, Ralph Waldo Emerson, Freud, and Marx, among so many others—were all preoccupied by the ways in which the appetite for money spoiled people's appetite for each other (and that that way madness lies). As the quest for wealth began to usurp all other quests—for redemption, for love, for equality, for justice, for truth—the desire for money began to transform people's sense of what it was to desire at all. This love of money was taken to be a very real threat to people's sanity. More and more people were possessed not simply by the necessary desire to survive, with some comfort, economically, but by the need for a surplus beyond their need that began to normalize a picture of human desiring as excessive, insatiable, unappeasable. Modern people needed more than they needed. Appetite as exorbitant was democratized. Frantic attempts were made to redescribe greed as not simply legitimate but morally impressive, a sign of character, of vitality. The rich person was living the best that life had to offer. Compared to money, even sex and nationalism and religion, even kindness and honesty, seemed like poor relatives. The "maddening money culture" produced a counterculture of extraordinary eloquence and inspiration, shell-shocked by the destructiveness of capitalism and hoping to bolster what Carlyle called "the sanity of nations." Societies based on commerce—that had transformed human wanting into an unprecedented wanting more—had to make wanting more quantifiable. People had to be calculating in new ways. "The psychological feature of our times," the sociologist Georg Simmel wrote in *The Philosophy of Money* (1900), was that, in an economy based on money, modern people could have an illusion of precision about what they wanted, and about what they wanted from each other. This feature, he writes,

> which stands in such a decisive contrast to the more impulsive, emotionally determined character of earlier epochs, seems to me to stand in a close causal relationship to the money economy. The money economy enforces the necessity of continuous mathematical operations in our daily transactions. The lives of many people are absorbed by such evaluating, weighing, cal-

culating and reducing of qualitative values to quantitative ones. Gauging values in terms of money has
taught us to determine and specify values down to the
last farthing and has thus enforced a much greater
precision in the comparison of various contents . . .
where they cannot be reduced to the common denom-
inator of money, a much more spontaneous evalua-
tion . . . is to be found.

In Simmel's account, money extends the empire of
quantification; not only does it make us think we can
quantify things that may not be suited to quantification
(like feelings, thoughts, moods, or desires), but it also lures
us into a desire for quantification, because of its apparent
benefits. Numbers are less ambiguous than words; and a
measurement is more obviously consensual than an im-
pression. But Simmel is describing something that works
its way into our minds, or rather something that seems to
describe how our minds work, what they are actually for;
that is, "evaluating, weighing, calculating and reducing of
qualitative values to quantitative ones." Once psychology
begins to legitimate itself as a science by developing
methods of measuring the mind—that is, by locating
something called the mind that has measurable things in
it, or that does things that are measurable—it is all too
easy for sanity and rationality to become virtually the

same thing. Quantification, and the calculation and control that seems to follow on from it, becomes the dominant metaphor. The sane are the people who can accurately calculate what they need and want; and who consent to the notion that human desiring is something, or rather is akin to things, that can be so measured. Madness is thus a new species of irrationality; the irrationality of inept assessment. By being made to look and sound quantifiable, human needing begins to be something that can be more or less efficient.

Once we think in terms of money, human needing shrinks in scope. We start to need only what we can calculate; we start to need as though all we need is money. "The desire for money," the philosopher Norman O. Brown wrote in *Life Against Death* (1959),

> takes the place of all genuinely human needs. Thus the apparent accumulation of wealth is really the impoverishment of human nature, and its appropriate morality is the renunciation of human nature and desires—asceticism. The effect is to substitute an abstraction, Homo economicus, for the concrete totality of human nature, and thus to dehumanize human nature. In this dehumanized human nature man loses contact with his own body, more specifically with his senses, with sensuality and with the pleasure-principle.

And this dehumanized human nature produces an in-human consciousness whose only currency is abstractions divorced from real life—the industrious, coolly rational, economic, prosaic mind. Capitalism has made us so stupid and one-sided that objects exist for us only if we can possess them, if they have utility.

Like Simmel, Brown is describing a state of possession; the way in which a powerful language gets inside us, and then seems to dictate to us who we really are. In Brown's terms we have fallen for the wrong story—or been hypnotized. The implication, as with Simmel, is that modern people, above all else, want to be distracted from the complexity of their needs. Whether it is called "continuous mathematical operations," or the "dehumanizing" or "impoverishment of human nature," needs must be reduced, or scaled down. And the deployment, explicitly or implicitly, of the language of mental health—spontaneity versus calculation, sensuous bodily desire versus abstraction—is recruited, as it always is, for a quasi-utopian, liberationist project. Money as the currency of human relations—talking in terms of whether people (or things) are worth it, and of what they are worth—reduces something we can call human nature to dispiriting proportions. It is not merely that it is mad to be rich, but that it may also be a form of madness to have consented to the language of money.

In the common currency of consoling fictions, the sane are deemed to be well-balanced (i.e., not excessive) and intelligible (i.e., we understand, more or less, what they are saying and doing, and what they are wanting). They don't puzzle us in ways that disturb us, nor are they extreme in ways that are disarming. As a group, one might say, they are singularly unthreatening. And not only are they unthreatening, they are also good to be around; in the imagined life the sane are a good influence. When Baby Warren, in Scott Fitzgerald's novel *Tender Is the Night* (1934), is discussing what to do with her mad sister, Nicole, she suggests to Nicole's husband, Dick, that they should go and live in London:

> ". . . the English are the best-balanced race in the world."
>
> "They are not," he disagreed.
>
> "They are. I know them, you see. I meant it might be nice for you to take a house in London for the spring season—I know a dove of a house in Talbot Square you could get, furnished. I mean living with sane, well-balanced English people."

Having good balance—and the picture of people as made up of feelings, say, or desires, or thoughts, that can be well or badly balanced—is a typical picture whenever sanity is discussed. But Baby Warren is, like her sister, Nicole, extremely rich; and is assuming, in her vulgarly naive way, that Nicole's sanity can effectively be bought. Sanity, like so much else in this novel about the financially booming 1920s in America, is assumed to be something that money can buy. Perhaps modern people can be balanced like books; in accounting for a person, their output can be matched by their input. And the sane and the mad are, of course, differentiated by what they are able (or willing) to take in, like food and love and sense and discipline; and what they give out, their words, their actions, their smell. "Better a sane crook than a mad puritan," Fitzgerald's narrator remarks later in the book, reminding us once again that it is appetite and transgression that are at stake when we are preferring the sane to the mad, or vice versa.

In achieving the right balance, or having a good balance, or becoming well-balanced, it is generally taken for granted that what can throw us off course are the wrong appetites, certain kinds of getting and spending. Even if what there is to balance, and the picture of good balance is contentious—assuming, for example, that the English in the 1920s were the best-balanced race—the picture of the mad as people who have lost their balance is compelling; as is the idea of sanity as a balancing act. This would once have been cast in the language of religion: in the language of sin and redemption we might have described how appetite undoes the well-being, the poise of a human being at her best. Baby might once have prescribed a religious or medical solution to her sister's woes. But now, so crude is the imagining of what sanity might be, she assumes that it is something that money can buy. And she is probably not alone now in assuming this.

PART three

Sane Now

A LL BLUEPRINTS OF what people should be like are at once denials of reality and attempts to create it anew. It is one of the peculiar characteristics of human wanting that it always involves being persuaded about what it is one should want. This persuasion, which takes many forms—from brainwashing to education, from seduction to conversation—is one way of describing the experience of growing up in any given society.

"People's social activities," the anthropologist Marhall Sahlins recently wrote in a letter to the *Times Literary Supplement*,

> including any that may be due to their genetic proclivities, are symbolically organized in diverse cultural ways. Not that the so-called instincts are lost, but that they come under conceptual definition, manipulation and control. Hence what is remarkable evolutionarily is not, for example, that all cultures have sex, but that

all sex has culture—varying from society to society in partners, occasions, locations, positions, and numerous ways of doing it. It can even be done by telephone.

The wanting without which human survival is impossible is symbolically organized; that is to say, wanting is inextricable from what it is our societies tell us we should want. If our loves and hates, our likings and our curiosities, our passions and our aversions "come under conceptual definition, manipulation and control," then there is no natural state in which we can live, or to which we can return. Indeed, the whole notion of a natural state, or a significant origin, is itself one of those culturally generated conceptual definitions. As, of course, are sanity and madness. They are symbolic organizations and representations of certain experiences in particular cultures. In our cultures you can do madness, as Sahlins says we can do sex, in various ways, although sanity doesn't seem to offer us quite so many positions. It is perhaps time to spell out what sanity could usefully be for us now; both what it would be like to be sane, and what being sane might involve us doing and feeling and wanting.

The twentieth century was a mass graveyard of idealistic, utopian projects for what was called in the eighteenth century the "perfectibility of man." We are living now in the aftermath of the horrifying consequences of politically designed Good Lives; of the most militant and coercive blueprints of what people should be and want and do with their lives. And it is not incidental that the languages of so-called mental health—of who is sane and who is mad—were so easily co-optable by fascists and communists alike. As ways of symbolically organizing who we should listen to and why, who should speak and who should be shut up and shut out, mental health becomes political morality by other means. Orwell's *1984* is our touchstone for the significance, political and otherwise, of the battle for the final definition of sanity. It is an important implication of *1984* that sanity and its definitions would not be so manipulable if they could be more freely and openly considered, if there were plans and guidelines for sanity that could be compared and contrasted. By keeping the debate so exclusively about madness, the mind doctors of the twentieth century, like the psychologists and moralists of the nineteenth century, have kept us (and themselves) in the dark about sanity. Designs for a good life, of which the whole notion of sanity must form a part, have been left to political theorists; and descriptions of the bad life, of a life lived in thrall to one of the many modern pathologies, have been left to neurologists, psychiatrists, and psychologists, the masters of modern mental health.

If there are madnesses, there should surely be sanities; and sanities that are not merely or simply the unlived lives of the supposedly sick and deranged. Sanities should be elaborated in the way that diagnoses of pathology are; they should be contested like syndromes, debated as to their causes and constitutions and outcomes, exactly as illnesses are. Taking as my motto Winnicott's remark that madness is the need to be believed, I want now to propose a blueprint for a contemporary sanity. I will describe what it is we should be wanting for ourselves in the name of sanity. And if the question is, for whom is this version of sanity being prescribed, the answer would be: for anyone who still wants to use the word; anyone who still gets some pleasure, some inspiration, however vague, from the idea of sanity. Anyone, that is to say, who is intrigued by Emerson's remark in his diary: "Sanity is very rare: every man almost and every woman has a dash of madness, and the combinations of society continually detect it. . . . Well a few times in history a well mixed character transpires. Look in the hundreds of persons each of us knows. Only a few whom we regard with great complacency, a few sanities." Or anyone who agrees with Leslie Farber's remark that, "Real talk between a man and a woman offers the supreme privilege of keeping the other sane, and being kept sane by the other," but doesn't really know why they intuitively assent to the statement. These are the people for whom a contemporary account of sanity might be of interest. Which is to say, perhaps, all of us. If the word itself is the merest piece of wish fulfillment, as reassuring as whistling in the dark, as consoling as secular prayer; if it is forged currency, a hoping against hope that we are not just what we call mad, it should be taken out of circulation so that we can work with what we have actually got, make do with what is really available to us. But we should also remember, both the disillusioned and the overimpressed alike, that sanity (unlike madness) has always needed rescuing. Our hope has always been that when we lose all sanity we can always find some more.

Sanity, then, as we have seen, is an antithetical word; it keeps opposites in play, it keeps alive our more haunting conflicts and confusions. It is in this sense more divided against itself, more at odds with itself, than it is with madness, its traditional antagonist. It shows us, at its most minimal, how ambivalent we are about wanting to be sane. And also how ambivalent we are about what we want sanity to mean. Sanity as a supposedly superficial quality is a caricature of normalcy. This sane person, viewed as a kind of cartoon character, is thoroughly reasonable, thoughtful, considerate, and well balanced; but he is also, by the same token, two-dimensional, soulless and uninspired, a triumph of conformism over idiosyncrasy. Sane here means so well adjusted as to have no character; so in apparent harmony with himself and others as to have no special life. For the superficially sane, sanity means a life without conflict, a life of relative peace, a life without malice or greed.

For the more deeply sane, whatever else sanity might be, it is a container of madness, not a denier of it. This sanity, again in its cartoon form, often bears the wisdom that accrues from hardships endured and conflicts forborne. This sane person has felt and acknowledged but not ultimately been overwhelmed by the rigors of his nature. His sanity, such as it is, is both the cause and the consequence of not having conformed, of discovering his true nature through a refusal to comply. For the superficially sane, adaptation is their religion; for the deeply sane, adaptation is what corrupts them, and is experienced as a form of submission. The deeply sane must not betray their desire; the superficially sane accommodate their desire to the needs of others. It is not incidental that sanity becomes a keyword in our societies in the nineteenth century, when questions of adaptation and compliance and privilege become the questions of the day. Sanity, then, is co-opted as either a form of resistance or a form of complicity with the powers that be. The version of sanity—Big Brother's version—that makes people biddable rather than willingly cooperative is regarded by the deeply sane as madness. Whether the sane are opportune or principled, serene or furious, inventive or dull, mechanical or inspired, indeed mad or sane, has always been open to debate. But the sane are never sadistic; they notably never get pleasure from cruelty.

The superficially sane are reassuring because they help us forget about madness; and because they are un-intimidated they are unintimidating. The deeply sane, like Lamb's genius, are all too mindful of madness, but they have its measure; they are impressive because they have never been overimpressed. The superficially sane are s[lick] while the deeply sane are rather more lik[e] heroines who have survived their [superficia]lly sane tend to convince us that [we are] our environments; arguing that if [you have the ri]ght upbringing and education, you will [be well] adjusted. The deeply sane, on the other hand, tell us that there is always more to us than our environments; that there is something within us—call it genius or a life force or instincts or genes—that exceeds the world that we find, and to which we must pay our most serious attention because it is driving us, one way or another, into what we are and will be. What we think sanity is, in other words, depends on how we describe what is inside us, on how we describe what we are made of. It is not surprising, perhaps, that in an era when such issues have never been so debated—or at least at a time when there have never been so many voices in the debate—that sanity has sounded less and less specific the more it is advocated.

The terms of this debate were spelled out in 1829, in Thomas Carlyle's famous, and appropriately entitled, essay "Signs of the Times." "Consider," he wrote,

> the great elements of human enjoyment, the attainments and possessions that exalt man's life to its present height, and see what part of these he owes to institutions, to Mechanism of any kind; and what to the instinctive, unbounded force which Nature herself lent him, and still continues to lend him. Shall we say, for example, that Science and Art are indebted principally to the founders of Schools and Universities? . . . On the whole institutions are much; but they are not all. The freest and highest spirits of the world have often been found under strange outward circumstances. . . . This we take it is the grand characteristic of our age. By our skill in mechanism, it has come to pass that in the management of external things we excel all other ages; while in whatever respects the pure moral nature, in true dignity of soul and character, we are perhaps inferior to most civilized ages.

What Carlyle calls "undue cultivation of the outward" we might call the technological manipulation of reality, treating the so-called inner world of feeling and desire as though it were the same as the external world. This is the official, consensual version of sanity (he calls it "Mechanism" because it is mechanistic, "synonymous with Logic, or the mere power of arranging and communicating"). And he contrasts Mechanism with Dynamism, the inner, spontaneous spring of life that as a Christian Romantic he thinks of as a moral force, like an inner voice. The Dynamic part of the self can neither join in nor fit in easily, and at its most extreme it thinks of joining in and fitting in as synonymous. Carlyle is skeptical enough to be all too mindful, though, of the excesses of Dynamism, which is itself akin to, if not a precursor of, what Laing called "true sanity." "Undue cultivation of the inward or Dynamical province leads to idle, visionary, impracticable courses," Carlyle writes,

> and, especially in rude eras, to Superstition and Fanaticism, with their long trail of baleful and well-known evils. Undue cultivation of the outward, again, though less immediately prejudicial, and even for the time productive of many palpable benefits, must, in the long run, by destroying Moral Force, which is the par-

ent of all other force, prove not less certainly and perhaps still more hopelessly, pernicious.

Sanity, Carlyle is saying, is a balancing of external
and internal influences. Too much external influence, too
much conforming to institutions—in the fullest sense of
family, state, school, university, and so on and on—and
we lose heart. Too little and we can feel unmoored from
our culture. The contemporary sane person may find
Carlyle's contraries, these sets of opposites, instructive,
but perhaps no longer fully satisfying. He will think of
these choices, between inner and outer, between improvi-
sation and compromise, between fitting in and joining in,
as an illusion of alternatives. Staged like this the drama is
too stark, too unnuanced, too either-orish to suit his new
needs and his new acknowledgment. His new needs are
organized around the fact that he lives as if he is exactly
the same as everyone else, and totally different at the
same time. His new acknowledgment is that his needs—
the ones he has learned that he has and the unsuspected
ones that could turn up or return at any moment—will
often be in conflict with each other; and will usually create conflict between himself and others. Sanity involves
learning to enjoy conflict, and giving up on all myths of
harmony, consistency, and redemption.

The sane person believes in order and pattern as at

best provisional, as a willfully false cure for inevitable change; and assumes that all stories about being saved or rescued are infantilizing alibis or blackmailing calculations. The sane, in other words, have nothing to complain about but a lot to do. Dissatisfaction is for them an inspiration rather than a refuge; they resist all inclinations to sulk or bear grudges, not because retreat and righteous accusation are themselves dispiriting and evidence of weakness of character, but because they have found ways of getting pleasure from the problems that these reactions are the poor solutions to. For the sane a sense of deprivation and a sense of wounded pride could never be redressed, or even addressed, by these or any other form of revenge. There are better ways of paying tribute to people than by taking revenge on them. Revenge is no good to the sane because it is an attempt to coerce agreement, in the form of submission and/or despair. Only people who don't expect to be listened to need people to agree with them, and the sane expect to be listened to. The sane prefer listening to speaking; indeed they regard most speaking as a defense against listening; though they realize, of course, what would happen in the unlikely situation of everyone wanting only to listen. After all, what would happen if everyone started listening at once?

The sane know that specialness—the need to be either only the chooser or the chosen—is a way of distract-

ing themselves from their own happiness. And that, iron-
ically perhaps, it has been their much cherished, their
most hallowed quest for self-knowledge—and for the self
that is the mock grail of the quest—that has been their
last-ditch attempt to perpetuate this sense of specialness,
of uniqueness, that is the secret saboteur of their liveliest
pleasures. Uniqueness is important only to people for
whom anonymity is a forbidden pleasure. For the sane
the need to be recognized, like the need to be understood, is unnecessary; they are in no need of rescue. It is
only for the unsane that rescue is unarguably better than
what they are being rescued from. The sane don't even
want to be one among many. What there is to be rescued
from is unmet need; being recognized, being desired, being seen, they all mean some kind of guarantee about not
being stranded in a flood of wants. Clearly, for a baby or
a child, to be ignored is to be abandoned. For the sane
adult—who is, by definition, not in thrall to the idea that
because she was once a child she is really a child—to be
ignored is one of her great freedoms. The search for
understanding is no more and no less than a fear of freedom for the sane adult; the wish to be known is a fear of
the unknown. Being desired, being recognized, being
understood—our favorite sliding scale—are useful for
some things, but not for others. The sane person wants
these things too, but in wanting them she is able to notice

what they can't do for her. If she tries to deprive herself of the experience of being left out—if she assumes that what you do when you are left out is just try to get back in—she will see so little of what there is outside that the unwitnessed life is left in abeyance, and solitariness is turned to taboo. The sane adult has not, in other words, consented to the modern redemptive myth of relationship; nor does she subscribe to the view that relationships are the kind of thing that one can be good or bad at, that one can succeed or fail at, any more than you can be good or bad at having red hair, or succeed or fail at being lucky. In the mixing and matching of two largely unknowable histories (of genetic endowment and personal experience), the only sane foregone conclusion about any relationship is that it is an experiment; and that exactly what it is an experiment in will never be clear to the participants. For the sane, so-called relationships could never be subject to contract.

For the sane the most compelling exchanges between people can never, in actuality, be subject to contract because sanity is lived according to acknowledgments, rather than principles; and these acknowledgments can never be formalized. I call them acknowledgments rather than principles because their consequences—or what they provide guidelines to—are at best ambiguous and, at even better, wholly indeterminate. The sane person's first acknowledgment is that her life is moved more by luck than by judgment; she sees her relationships as coincidences rather than destinies, her talents as unearned gifts, her bodily life as genetically contingent, her parents as giving her a good or a bad chance, and so on. The only necessities her life has are the ones she ascribes to them. The second acknowledgment of the sane is that they are, peculiarly, animals who are often unconscious of what they want; and that some of the wants they are most conscious of serve to obscure their keener satisfactions. And this is because their third acknowledgment is that what they most want they must not have because it is forbidden them (this is what the incest taboo is there to manage).

So the sane have a sense that anything they want is either going to frustrate them because it isn't quite what they really want; or it is going to horrify them because it is more nearly what they want, and so they will be unable to enjoy it. The sane, in other words, are ironic rather than fanatical in their pleasure seeking (and one of the things they are most slyly amused by is just how earnest and hypochondriacal the committed hedonists always are). From this point of view "we" are never, strictly speaking, out of control or being excessive, we are simply doing forbidden things. The sane acknowledge that real pleasure seeking is extremely risky, but won't use this acknowledgment as a refuge from actually taking the requisite risks, which are the ones that, if one fails to take, one loses one's pleasure in oneself. For the sane adult, security only sustains the appetite for security.

The overprotected child is always wondering what must be out there that he needs so much protection from; the underprotected child is always wondering, to begin with, where his parents are, and then where he is himself in all this armor he has had to put on. The sane parents can never get protecting their child right; indeed don't think of parenting as something that one can get right, but as something that one muddles through. The sane parent knows that being a child means being unprepared for life, and so needing a parent in order to live it; but the sane parent also knows that life is not exactly the kind of thing that can be prepared for. For a child growing up, life is by definition full of surprises; the adult tries to keep these as surprises, rather than as traumas, through a devoted attentiveness. But sane parenting always involves a growing sense of how little, as well as how much, one can protect one's child from; of just how little a life can be programmed. Sane parents do not invent their children, they just create the conditions in which they might grow.

The sane adult is protective—and not only of children, but of himself and others—in a way that avoids covertly undermining the strengths of those who are apparently in need of protection ("The friends of the born nurse/ Are always getting worse," as W. H. Auden wrote). The sane adult assumes that it is possible for people to get pleasure from who they happen to be, and that part of this pleasure is bound up with versions of self-reliance that are not merely a more or less bitter denial of a need for other people. The two most dispiriting forms of modern relationship are the protection racket and the sadomasochistic contract in which, respectively, one person's strength depends on the other person's weakness, or one person's pleasure depends on the other person's suffering. The sane person's project is to find more appealing ways of being weak and strong; or to find alternative pleasures to the pleasures of power and of helplessness. The way most people are prone to see what they call human nature now makes even the thought of alternative forms of pleasure and excitement sound hopelessly naive. It would be part of the sane person's sanity to want new forms of pleasure in which neither one's kindness nor one's excitement are overly compromised (one emblem of this might be those gay men who experiment in coming without getting an erection). The sane person knows that being able to only be a nice person is the death of sexual excitement; and that being able to only be nasty is too isolating.

In sane sex the main preoccupation is to not protect

oneself and the other person from one's appetite; and the primary acknowledgment is that one's appetite is born of a strange interweaving of one's history and temperament, and that both its expression and its consequences are unpredictable. Who one desires and is desired by is always going to be at once unfathomable and strangely intelligible; the new person, as someone out of the echo chamber of one's history, feels surprisingly familiar, yet the new person, as someone from the unknown, is nothing but a stranger.

We recognize sexual desire by the fact that once again—once again, after childhood—we feel our safety and our excitement are in conflict with each other. When we feel we are taking a risk, or are at risk, there is always an object of desire in the vicinity. In sane sex one cannot afford to sacrifice too much of one's excitement to one's security, because the sacrifice of excitement is the royal road to envy and resentment (and its self-cure, depression). One cannot afford to be too self-knowing in one's pursuit of pleasure, because it is the sacrifice of self-recognition that sponsors forbidden pleasure. If pleasure is forbidden, we need the illusion of the unknown when we pursue it. As there is no appetite, sexual or otherwise, without excitement, the sane person has to be unusually mindful of all the ways she has of attacking, trivializing, ignoring, ironizing, and generally spoiling her own excitement. So she will prize charm in herself and others because charm gives excitement a chance; and she will be suspicious of her own shyness—and more sympathetically suspicious of other people's—because it too smugly keeps the excited self at bay.

For the sane person, whether or not hearts are made to be broken, selves are made to be lost, and this simply means noting that what we tend to call ourselves or our characters are both threatened and strengthened by excitement. In sex with other people we can lose ourselves; in masturbation we can consolidate ourselves. It is always only the other person who can introduce us to a new pleasure; and by the same token it is only by ourselves that we can refine—rejoin and replay—our old familiar pleasures. The sane person relishes both experiences because she takes it for granted that our personal history is encoded in and expressed by our sexuality; and all our histories are an alternation of private and shared pleasures. The sane person believes that sharing cannot be taught, it can only be desired; when sharing is an obligation, it is an aggression against the other person. Sharing sex reveals so much more about one's history—to oneself and the other person—than telling stories about one's childhood. It is, in this sense, so radically self-exposing of a person's wants and fears and shames and whims that it should not be surprising that we are inclined to think of sex as private. One way the sane person gets around this is by not consenting to the modern belief that the most interesting, the most important, the most defining thing about a person is his history. Indeed, the sane person is on the lookout for stories that are not family stories; for the ways modern people have found of inhabiting their histories in different ways. It would be sane now to wonder, for example, whether there are any alternatives to nostalgia, or the malign nostalgia that is blame, in our uses of the past. Whether there are stories we can tell about ourselves that are not stories about the past. And the new sane person wants to be able to do this because he needs a new story about kindness. All the old stories are about cruelty, which might suggest to us that people aren't really very nice. Whereas it seems more likely to the sane person that we have so far come up with stories about goodness that give badness all the best lines. It is imperative, given his impoverished history—how silly, how enervated he tends to look when compared with the mad—that the truly sane person has ways of being good, and of talking about goodness or kindness, that aren't just another opportunity to make us feel more ashamed and more sorry for ourselves. Stories about kindness are traditionally about our falling short. That we think of ourselves now as the kind of creatures who want a humiliating morality is a part of our morality. We know ourselves most happily as diminished things. The sane want to know whether we can really love anything other than the bad news about ourselves.

The bad news about ourselves is about appetite, about sexuality and destructiveness; and what we have called madness has always been the voicing of, or the self-cure for, these extreme energies that we feel to be driving us. We may want to be kinder, but what is driving us cares all too little about this particular want; as if we aren't what we should be, but what we think we should be has all too little to do with who we actually are. Morality becomes the word for having got the wrong idea about ourselves, about what kind of animals we are. And this is when, as we have seen, sanity comes in as a reassuring picture so that we can, at least occasionally, either be at one with our nature, or in noble and ennobling conflict with it. Sanity here means harmony, or the supreme bearing of conflict. Whereas the mad, in their complementary way, are either in disarray or in excessive conflict with themselves and others, creating havoc in their attempts to abolish conflict (the logic being: if you eradicate the enemy, the battle will be over).

So if, for example, it is conventionally kind and therefore sane not to attack or punish or exploit people's vulnerabilities—"we" tend to think of people who rape or murder children, or who torture the sick or the old, as mad—in war it is the nature of the project to do exactly that. If the sane person lives as if cruelty is the worst thing she does, then no sane person could win a war. The sane person has to give an account of just what it would be to be kind in a war; or she has to come up with an alternative to the basic model of a person as a war; or she has to come up with a more ample, a more inclusive picture that acknowledges that a person is a war (is at war) but that a person is also many other things beside. The sane person accepts that a person is a war, but finds this too bewitching and therefore too limiting. One would be wildly out of touch with reality not to see war everywhere; but one could also get too addicted to one picture of reality.

The sane would not think it was worth dying for anybody's sentences, including their own. Instead of being profoundly moved by the idea of sacrifice, they are profoundly suspicious of it; indeed, if their skepticism is for anything, it is for all the ways we have been educated and seduced and cajoled into believing that our capacity for sacrifice, whether of self and/or others, is one of the best things about us. It would be the first principle of the sane kindness that all forms of sacrifice would be avoided, if at all possible. And following on from this, the second principle of sane kindness is that no adult can know what's best for another adult; and, by the same token, no group or society can know what's best for another group or society. Adults are the ones who are supposed to know what's best for children (quite soon, of course, the children start answering back); it is the oppressive legacy, more insidious than is often noticed, of using parents and children as the model for what goes on between adults that adults begin to behave like parents to other adults. Sane adult kindness involves finding out, one way or another, what the other person thinks is best for her, and then making a choice; no sane adults can know in any absolute sense what is best for them, but no sane kind adults could claim to know others better than they know themselves. They could claim to know them in other ways than they know themselves, but not in better ways. And, by the same token, no sane, kind person can accept a description of another person as in any sense true if that person herself does not accept it.

The sane, kind person believes that getting on with people (including oneself) is more important than knowing or understanding people. That, in fact, if knowing or understanding people has a point, it is that it is in the service of getting on with them. For the sane person good manners can only possibly mean being a genial person;

and the enemy of geniality, of the kind of sociability that makes people feel better, is the excessive need to be special. Struck by just how frightened people are of each other, and not always with good reason, the sane do what they can to be unimpressed by intimidation. The sane, in other words, could never seek reassurance in the prestige of others; reassurance could come only from those things held in common (i.e., having been children, living out a largely unknown history, being subject to illness and accident, aging and death and their attendant anxieties, and so on). Because the sane know that everyone is anxious all the time, they also know that everyone needs reassurance, especially those who claim to loathe it. Because the sane love wishes and are sufficiently interested in reality, they have to be at their most artful in the giving of reassurance; if it's too wishful, it's poor equipment and doesn't mobilize the person's resources; if it's too realistic, it frightens them out of their wits, which they need. The sane believe that fear is a great educator, but a bad master; and that all suffering is bad, but that some suffering is unavoidable. For the sane person, above all, a kind act can ultimately be defined as kind only by the recipient; for the sane, good intentions are not even half the battle. The sane believe that the only thing that matters about so-called intentions is their consequences.

Just as, for the sane, everyone is bisexual because

everyone has had a mother and a father (absent and/or present) whom they have loved and desired and hated, everyone is also free to pursue their sexual inclinations, not simply as long as they don't harm other people, but as long as they don't harm other people in ways that they don't want to be harmed. The kindest thing a sane adult can do is assume that other people can make choices, while being mindful of the areas of people's lives in which choice does not apply. (I can't choose who I desire or fall in love with; I can't choose whether what I plant will grow.) So the sane don't use words such as "self-control" or "self-discipline," or "effort" or "willpower"; they talk instead of "temptation" and the doing and the not doing of "forbidden" things. The sane choose to do forbidden things because they sense that the thing they want to do is forbidden. They don't use these traditional phrases because they don't picture people as creatures who are always potentially out of control, any more than any other animal is (rabid dogs one could honestly say were out of control). They don't picture people as bad and struggling to be good; but as having strong, competing wants, and wanting to stay alive into the bargain.

So instead of sanity as seeming to be a choice between conformity and self-assertion, between sincerity and authenticity, between duty and desire, the sane person would want, ideally, to incorporate each of these into a repertoire rather than make the grand gesture of choosing between them. Each, in different circumstances, might be useful; one needs to be able to lie to the Gestapo and tell the truth to one's friend. One needs to conform to the rules of football in order to play it; and only by conforming to the rules can one excel. It should, perhaps, be rather more of a duty than a desire to visit one's aging parents. It would be sane now not to be the emperor of one idea; to start from the position that everyone is right from their own point of view; and to take it for granted that everyone is even more confused than they seem. Havoc is always wreaked in fast cures for confusion. The sane believe that confusion, acknowledged, is a virtue; and that humiliating another person is the worst thing we ever do. Sanity should not be our word for the alternatives to madness; it should refer to whatever resources we have to prevent humiliation.

ALSO BY
ADAM PHILLIPS

SIDE EFFECTS

ISBN ISBN 978-0-00-715538-5
(paperback)

Psychoanalysis as a form of therapy works by attending to the patient's side effects, that is, "what falls out of his pockets once he starts speaking." Undergoing psychoanalytic treatment is in many ways like reading a powerful work of literature—a leap into the dark. It's impossible to know beforehand the effect it will have. All we can do, as the essays in this book suggest, is see where the side effects will lead us.

"[Phillips] is the closest thing we have to a philosopher of happiness."   —*The Observer*

"Phillips is one of the finest prose stylists at work in the language, an Emerson for our time."   —John Banville

"[*Side Effects*] is . . . a remarkably comprehensive and stimulating overview of contemporary psychoanalytical thinking as well as a supremely confident restating of the Freudian conception of life and life's vicissitudes."—*Irish Times*

"These essays . . . are vintage Phillips: enlightening and intelligent; dynamic and delectably interdisciplinary."   —*Time Out*

For more information about upcoming titles, visit www.harperperennial.com.

Visit www.AuthorTracker.com
for exclusive information on your favorite HarperCollins authors.

Available wherever books are sold, or call 1-800-331-3761 to order.

HARPER ● PERENNIAL